Southern Literary Studies
Louis D. Rubin, Jr., Editor

*Mary Lee Settle's Beulah Quintet*

# *Mary Lee Settle's Beulah Quintet*

## The Price of Freedom

Brian Rosenberg

Louisiana State University Press
Baton Rouge and London

Manufactured in the United States of America
First printing
00 99 98 97 96 95 94 93 92 91 5 4 3 2 1

Designer: Glynnis Phoebe
Typeface: Galliard
Typesetter: Graphic Composition, Inc.
Printer and binder: Thomson-Shore, Inc.

Library of Congress Cataloging-in-Publication Data

Rosenberg, Brian, 1955–
Mary Lee Settle's Beulah quintet : the price of freedom / Brian Rosenberg.
p. cm. —(Southern literary studies)
Includes bibliographical references (p. ) and index.
ISBN 0-8071-1674-2
1. Settle, Mary Lee. Beulah quintet. 2. Historical fiction, American—History and criticism. 3. West Virginia in literature.
I. Title. II. Series.
PS3569.E84B4837 1991
813′.54—dc20 91-8264
CIP

The author is grateful to the editor of the *Virginia Quarterly Review* for permission to reprint material from his essay "Mary Lee Settle and the Critics," which first appeared in that journal's Volume LXV (1989), 401–17. The author also makes use of material that originally appeared in his essay "Mary Lee Settle and the Tradition of Historical Fiction," *South Atlantic Quarterly,* LXXXVI (1987), 229–43; and "The Price of Freedom: An Interview with Mary Lee Settle," *Southern Review,* n.s., XXV (Spring, 1989), 351–65, which he edited.

The paper in this book meets the guidelines for permanence and durability of the Committee on Production Guidelines for Book Longevity of the Council on Library Resources.♾

*To Carol*

# Contents

# Preface

"The Beulah Quintet does not fit"—the opening to Roger Shattuck's essay on Mary Lee Settle—might be taken as an epigraph for this study, whose primary purpose is to investigate why Settle's series of historical novels does or does not "fit" into a variety of contexts, categories, and traditions.[1] Its relations to the evolution of historical fiction in both America and Europe are complex and, I shall argue, unique; its role in the development of contemporary fiction, and particularly in the development of women's fiction, has been problematic; and its impact on the popular and academic reading publics has been curious and difficult to gauge. Nearly as interesting as the quintet itself, in my view one of the major works of modern American fiction, are some of the questions raised by its coming into existence. From one perspective it might be seen as the inevitable product of recent trends in narratology, historiography, and American studies; from another it might be seen as arising out of nowhere, puzzling and idiosyncratic. From any perspective it must be seen as one of the few grandly ambitious works of historical fiction written by an American woman.

The argument at the center of this book is that the Beulah quintet represents an attempt to apply a European tradition of historical re-creation to American experience and to adapt a largely conservative

1. Roger Shattuck, Introduction to *The Beulah Quintet* (New York, 1981), vii.

form to the demands of a revolutionary history and ideology. Settle, in other words, brings the methods of Walter Scott, George Eliot, and Leo Tolstoy to bear upon the land of Ralph Waldo Emerson, Henry David Thoreau, and Herman Melville. And while the immediate subject of her novels is the history of a region in West Virginia, the broader subject is the evolution of the beliefs, conflicts, principles, and illusions that gave rise to and continue to distinguish American culture. Necessarily, since Settle's is a revisionist history, she has replaced a number of prevalent American myths with what she considers historical truth and, in some cases, with alternative myths more accurately reflective of American reality. Of particular concern to her are the relations between the empowered and the powerless, or the dispossessors and the dispossessed, that is, between wealthy and impoverished, governing and rebellious, Anglo-Saxon and non-Anglo-Saxon, male and female. As important as the history Settle relates is the one she deconstructs.

A second argument, developed primarily at the start of the book, has to do with the reception of the quintet, which clearly is not among the canonical works of contemporary American literature. That this should be the case is unsurprising, given the relative smallness and instability of the contemporary canon; why it should be the case is, nonetheless, interesting and revelatory, to the extent that virtually every critic who has written about Settle has been drawn to speculate about her reputation. As recent studies of the canon from feminist, nonwhite, and other perspectives have shown, it is often easier to identify the forces at work in establishing literary value by examining a marginalized rather than a mainstream text. What appears absolute when one is evaluating a "classic" may become obviously less so when one is evaluating a work denied classic status. Because the Beulah quintet runs counter to so many currents in contemporary literary studies, the novels cast those currents into relief and become a means of understanding the biases and priorities that direct the reading public and the academy. Even if one wishes to avoid a defensive tone, it becomes difficult to speak about the strengths of the quintet without remarking on why these strengths have yet to be widely acknowledged.

The largest portion of this book is devoted to readings of *Prisons, O Beulah Land, Know Nothing, The Scapegoat,* and *The Killing Ground* and especially to an analysis of the themes, images, and habits of language that unify the separate novels into a larger whole. Although each narrative is in most obvious ways self-sufficient and though variations in style and substance must be expected among texts composed over a period of twenty-six years, I will generally be assuming that each novel is best read as an installment in a single, continuous fiction of better than fifteen hundred pages. This assumption reflects not only Settle's own claims about the quintet but the experience of readers who come to the later volumes without knowledge of the earlier and leave disappointed or confused. Read together and in sequence, the novels are more coherent and, especially, more ironic than when read independently; apparently meaningless objects are shown to be symbols, assumptions made by characters to be comically or tragically erroneous, and individual actions to be recurrent parts of a larger familial or national pattern. Proceeding through the quintet, one gradually becomes wiser and more historically knowledgeable than most of the characters and therefore increasingly able to judge and contextualize their behavior.

While this study is not an introduction to the Beulah quintet, finally, in the sense that it does not dwell at length on background material and plot summary, it has been affected by the relative contemporaneity and obscurity of its subject. I have assumed less familiarity with the texts under discussion than I might had I been writing about Melville or Charles Dickens. Analytic and descriptive passages are interwoven so that, as far as possible, the reader can be told simultaneously about the subject, shape, and underlying intentions of each novel. Periodically I interrupt the consideration of individual works with fairly general characterizations of Settle's tendencies as a writer. One consequence of writing about a noncanonical author is the need continually to remember the limited size of the informed audience and the importance of summarizing and contextualizing. Another, at once more intimidating and liberating, is the need to engage a series of texts without the mediating influence of an extensive body of criticism. For better or worse, criticism takes on a different character when the study of a particular writer or work becomes commonplace and institutionalized. Answers to some of the most basic questions—questions about value, suitability for study, historical importance, and so on—are taken for granted, and nearly every new critical assessment becomes a revision of earlier ones.

Given the scarcity of relevant books and articles, virtually everything said by the critic of Mary Lee Settle will be said in print for the first time. Although this newness is no guarantee that the discourse will be any more or less helpful or interesting, it is likely to influence subjects, tone, and rhetorical strategies: released from the need to participate in a vast competitive chorus, the critic is left to contemplate the sound of his own voice.

I should remark briefly on my decision to include the interview with Mary Lee Settle as an appendix to the critical portion of this volume. Such a juxtaposition is rarely attempted, on the supposition, presumably, that critical judgments are liable to be distorted or contaminated by being brought into proximity with authorial intentions and opinions. This assumption, derived largely from New Critical and structuralist approaches to the relations between the text and its creator, is one I have, for a number of reasons, chosen not to accept. In practical terms, the interview is an essential secondary source to which readers of this book should be able readily to refer. It is cited here so frequently and drawn upon for so much information about textual history and theoretical orientation that its easy availability is virtually as important as the availability of the novels in the quintet. Some sections of the interview have appeared in no other printed form.

On another level, the inclusion of the interview indicates my conviction that authorial intentions must be taken into account when one is constructing the meaning of any literary work. In general I share, and would expand to include all forms of art, Jerome McGann's belief that "the expressed intentions, or purposes, of an author are . . . significant for understanding a poem." McGann explains their significance in this way: "At the point of origin those intentions are codified in the author's choice of time, place, and form of publication—or none of the above, by which I mean his decision *not* to publish at all, or to circulate in manuscript, or to print privately. All such decisions take the form of specific social acts of one sort or another, and those acts enter as part of the larger social act which is the poem in its specific (and quite various) human history." He adds, "What we call 'author intentions' all appear in his particular statements about his own work."[2] Although

2. Jerome J. McGann, *The Beauty of Inflections: Literary Investigations in Historical Method and Theory* (New York, 1988), 23–24.

these statements do not determine the meaning of a work, they do become part of the process by which that meaning is determined, that is, by which the work is seen in the context of a particular time or society or group of ideologies. This process becomes especially important in a study, like this one, that attempts to situate a work in relation to a set of generic, cultural, and historical categories. My readings of the Beulah quintet are not bound by Settle's expressions of purpose and at times, in fact, come into conflict with them, but they are consistently informed by an awareness of those expressions.

The interview, finally, provides the reader with an interesting opportunity to judge and contextualize my own critical agenda. Again I quote McGann: "Like its own object of study ('literature'), criticism is necessarily 'tendentious' in its operations." This precept suggests that the critic and, even more, the reader of criticism must "take careful account of all contextual factors that impinge on the critical act" and shape its implicit aims and assumptions.[3] To a degree one automatically does this accounting when reading criticism by comparing the critic's response to a work to one's own and locating in the difference the personality and cultural situation of the critic. I am simply providing the reader with an additional point of comparison. Measuring my response to expressions of authorial intent against the expressions themselves may reveal the (unavoidable) tendentiousness of the criticism more clearly, or even differently, than do claims in the criticism itself.

The inclination after completing a first book is to thank virtually everyone who has shaped, however slightly or unknowingly, one's personal history. That inclination I will resist, at least in print. Special thanks, however, are due to Joshua Hanft, who introduced me to the fiction of Mary Lee Settle; to Allegheny College, for generously supporting in a variety of ways my work on this project; to many of my colleagues at Allegheny but especially my friends James Bulman, Lloyd Michaels, and Susan Smith, for their wisdom and reassurance; to Mary Lee Settle, for her extraordinary patience and generosity; to my family; and, most emphatically, to Dr. Carol Anzalone Rosenberg, who has always (against her better interests, I fear) encouraged me to follow my heart.

3. *Ibid.,* 25.

*Mary Lee Settle's Beulah Quintet*

# Settle and the Critics: The Politics of Reputation 1

The urge among all who study a neglected writer is to justify the writer's historical and literary importance and, by implication, the importance of the act of critical valorization in which the student is engaged. No matter whether the book be *Frankenstein* or *Varney the Vampire:* the justification is likely to be impassioned and, I suspect, to make little impact on readers either unfamiliar with the text in question or familiar enough to have already formed and grown attached to judgments of their own. Those who admire *Varney* will applaud the novel's new advocate; those who do not will, at best, tolerate the eccentricity of his taste. The tendency to champion an overlooked or underappreciated author and at the same time to chastize the responsible popular, critical, or academic community has been particularly common during the past few years, when the literary canon has come to be recognized, at least by some, as a product of political and ideological choices and has been attacked and redefined from a variety of cultural and theoretic perspectives. Our bookstores, and our journal articles as well, are filled with rediscovered "classics" and little-known "masterpieces."

My purpose in this study is not to rail against either the highbrow or lowbrow readers who have paid little attention to Mary Lee Settle but to detail the qualities of mind that have shaped her historical fiction and to explore the relations between her novels and a set of influential traditions. There is, however, no point in ignoring the widespread indifference that has been the prevailing response to her considerable body of work. The history of that response is worth examining because it reveals much about the process by which popular and especially academic judgments are formed. What is surprising, really, about Settle's audience is not that it has been so unduly small but that its undue smallness is in retrospect so easy to explain. If one set out to create a novelist both artistically imposing and little read, one might end by creating Mary Lee Settle.

Actually, the response to Settle's first two books carries little warning of any subsequent neglect, just as the novels themselves seem in few obvious ways preparatory to the more ambitious novels that follow. *The Love Eaters,* published in 1954, and *The Kiss of Kin,* which appeared in 1955, are compact, bitterly ironic examples of contemporary social realism, more reminiscent of works by Angus Wilson or Evelyn Waugh than of fiction either American or historical. Both were widely and on the whole favorably reviewed in England and the United States, and the selection of *The Kiss of Kin* as a Book-of-the-Month-Club Alternate seemed to anticipate a career of at least moderate popular success. The consistency of opinion among the reviewers is noteworthy. Aside from the formulaic testimonies to the promise of the beginning novelist, their most frequent subject is the deftness, relevance, and almost painful accuracy of her social vision—a vision described again and again, in language of sometimes astonishing violence, as raw, acidic, vicious, relentless, and, in at least four different reviews, sharp. The one hint of Settle's later difficulty in attracting readers comes in the reluctant, almost oxymoronic quality of this early praise: her novels are described as "morbidly fascinating," "uncomfortably alive," and "unpleasant [but] true" and, in a memorable phrase, as fiction steeped in "wholesome acids."[1]

This relative unanimity of response disappeared when Settle pub-

1. Quotations, phrases, and descriptive terms about the works have been drawn from the following reviews. *The Love Eaters:* F. A. Boyle, *Library Journal,* LXXX (1955), 885; John Raymond, *New Statesman and Nation,* XLVII (1954), 737; unsigned review in *New York Herald Tribune Book Review,* July 24, 1955, p. 6; Richard McLaughlin, Springfield *Republican,* April 17, 1955, p. 10; unsigned review in *Times Literary Supplement,* May 21, 1954, p. 325. *The Kiss of Kin:* unsigned review in *Kirkus,* XXIII (1955), 813; Walter Allen, *New Statesman and Nation,* XLIX (1955), 146; unsigned review in *Saturday Review,* February 18, 1956, p. 54.

lished *O Beulah Land* in 1956. Most striking about the reviews of that novel and of *Know Nothing,* published in 1960, is the radical difference between the reception of Settle the contemporary ironist and Settle the writer of (still ironic) southern historical fiction. Settle herself seems to have become aware of the change in response almost immediately. "I was an acerbic young novelist getting a great deal of praise, and suddenly I was writing a historical novel," she recalls. "The noses turned up all over the place, and I lost what reputation I was building" (Appendix B, p. 160). "Had she chosen to continue to write . . . about modern people and problems in recognizable contemporary settings," George Garrett speculates, "there would, it seems, have been a safe and secure place, if not an especially distinguished one, for her in the literary scene."[2]

The reviews of the historical fiction, positive and negative, share a sometimes tacit, sometimes explicit regret that so talented a novelist chose to work in so debased a form and argue either that she managed to transcend its ordinary limitations or that she has contributed yet another to a long series of "blowzy Technicolored so-called historical romances." Some favorable reviews seem less concerned with praising Settle's fiction than with castigating, in the strongest possible terms, other historical novels of the time: *O Beulah Land* "is head and shoulders above most of its contemporaries" and "ranks far above the formula-ridden and sensational historical novels that have misrepresented American history in recent years." *Know Nothing* is "a welcome contrast to the mass of . . . historical romances designed for those who prefer to read lying down"; if "books which bury the past beneath a weight of verbiage bring historical fiction into disrepute," this novel helps "reinstate it." Other reviews are so awash in contempt for the genre that praise and condemnation are almost impossible to separate: *O Beulah Land* "can be appreciated by those who prefer their history like their breakfast cereal—sugar-coated"; it is "a sound historical novel suited to the taste of men, women, and some young people who want more than just blood, thunder, and bosoms in their reading about the past." And *Know Nothing* provides sustenance "for those voracious readers who must read everything about the Civil War, and for those

2. George Garrett, *Understanding Mary Lee Settle* (Columbia, S.C., 1988), 84–85.

who have never gotten over *Gone with the Wind.*" Somehow, in the minds of the reviewers, the shift from the twentieth to the eighteenth and nineteenth centuries thoroughly neutralized the wholesomely acidic qualities of Settle's earlier work.[3]

Clearly the effects of Settle's categorization as a writer of mere historical fiction were lingering. None of her next three novels—*Fight Night on a Sweet Saturday,* which appeared in 1964, *The Clam Shell,* published in 1971, and *Prisons,* which came out in 1973—received nearly the attention given her initial four (only the first, for instance, is even listed in *Book Review Digest*), and all moved out of print very quickly. Even the winning of the National Book Award for Fiction by *Blood Tie* in 1978, an event that Garrett calls "a turning point in at least the public aspect of her life's work," initially provoked more complaints about the nature of literary awards than plaudits for Settle, the tangential literary-political issue overshadowing the achievement of the novelist.[4] Still, largely because of the stature conferred by the award, Settle's next two novels, *The Scapegoat* and *The Killing Ground,* published in 1980 and 1982, respectively, managed to be reviewed in more prominent places (the front page of the *New York Times Book Review*), by more prominent persons (E. L. Doctorow, Gail Godwin), and certainly in more flattering terms ("[*The Scapegoat*] is as good a novel as anyone writing in this country today could have written").[5] The Beulah quintet began to be reissued in a new paperback series, though, characteristically, publishing problems prevented all five volumes from being released in the same format by the same press.

3. Quotations about the works have been drawn from the following reviews. *O Beulah Land:* Melvin Maddocks, *Christian Science Monitor,* September 6, 1956, p. 5; Lyn Hart, *Library Journal,* LXXXI (1956), 2000; Charlotte Capers, *New York Times Book Review,* September 9, 1956, p. 5; Carl Carmer, *Saturday Review,* September 15, 1956, p. 21. *Know Nothing:* Lyn Hart, *Library Journal,* LXXXV (1960), 3105; William Peden, *Saturday Review,* November 5, 1960, p. 33; Olivia Manning, *Spectator,* October 13, 1961, p. 514.

4. George Garrett, "Mary Lee Settle," in *Dictionary of Literary Biography,* 2nd ser. (Detroit, 1980), 282.

5. Robert Houston, Review of *The Scapegoat,* in *Nation,* November 8, 1980, p. 469. Both Doctorow, in Review of *The Scapegoat,* in *New York Times Book Review,* October 26, 1980, pp. 1, 40–42, and Godwin, in Review of *The Killing Ground,* in *New Republic,* XVI (1982), 30–31, were highly complimentary, as were other reviewers, including Rosellen Brown and J. D. O'Hara. Doctorow's review, frequently cited by Settle's critics and publishers, is probably the most insightful yet written about her work.

At the beginning of the nineties, Settle seems to have reached a state of equilibrium as far as the popular press and the publishing industry are concerned, having moved from promising newcomer to proven veteran without ever experiencing a period of real acceptance. Although her older novels, including the quintet, have once again been reissued (this time by Scribner's) in paperback, the republication was not supported by a significant advertising campaign and has received, at least to this point, relatively little attention. *Celebration,* which came out in 1986 and is among Settle's most accessible novels, was widely, if not prominently, reviewed in respectful terms; *Charley Bland,* published in 1989, fared somewhat better, though it appears not to have provoked in the short term a dramatic shift in popular or critical response. The early reviews of the novel, tellingly, emphasize the beauty of its prose and the distinctly southern character of its story. Sybil Steinberg's review in *Publishers Weekly* is typical: "A familiar story, perhaps, but Settle recounts it in beautifully cadenced, lyrical prose, her elegaic tone perfectly sustained, her ironic insights stinging with her special understanding of how Southern codes of conduct . . . foreordain the tragic waste of lives."[6] If Settle is to become more widely known, it will be, I suspect, primarily as a southern writer and not as a writer of historical fiction. The former label is at the moment far more respectable.

Essentially a novelist can achieve something larger than limited reknown in two ways: by reaching a broad popular audience or by impressing the literary establishment, in one manner or another, sufficiently to be considered important literature, by which I mean appealing to what Terry Eagleton identifies as "the largely concealed structure of values" that informs such cultural determinations. If we leave aside for the moment questions of merit, it seems clear that Settle's work has been ill-suited to either channel of acceptance. Her historical fiction bears almost no resemblance to the sort that has for the last several decades been widely read; the tendency of some reviewers to liken her novels to the conventional historical romance has rather been compelling testimony to the power of expectation to shape one's experience of a text ("Here we have another novel set in the antebellum

6. Sybil Steinberg, Review of *Charley Bland,* in *Publishers Weekly,* June 23, 1989, p. 50.

South"). Nor is the density of her novels such that they would appeal to the general reading public. "Wherever one places Settle in the literary spectrum," notes Peggy Bach, "she cannot be accused of writing easy reading."[7] All of her novels, but particularly those of the quintet, can be demanding to the point of frustration. Works so populated as these are by huge casts of named characters (*O Beulah Land,* for instance, contains nearly three dozen) ordinarily arrange them into groups of clearly differentiated importance, with carefully developed protagonists surrounded by less fully rendered figures playing secondary or tertiary roles. Many of Settle's characters, though, are pictured with equivalent care, play roles of roughly equal importance, and move in and out of the text unpredictably, now occupying the center of the frame, now vanishing altogether. The expected hierarchy breaks down, and the familiar devices for ordering, judging, and recalling characters are of little use.

Similar liberties are taken with plot and point of view. Because, in most of the novels, different characters are of primary importance at different times, plot consists not of a central tale surrounded by others of lesser prominence but of a collection of stories woven together into a complex narrative fabric. Point of view, often tied in Settle to the consciousness of the character currently central, may shift abruptly from first to third person and from one level of omniscience or reliability to another. Even a first-person narrative such as *Prisons* will glide almost without warning from 1649 to 1634 and from the perspective of an adult to the perspective of the same adult seeing again through his own eyes as a child. The effect of this shifting has been likened to the experience of reading William Faulkner, viewing a tapestry, looking through a kaleidoscope, watching an elaborate folk dance, but never, by those who read Settle carefully, to the effect of conventional narrative.[8]

Additional demands are placed on the reader by the unusual complexities of Settle's prose. Her intention in each of the historical novels

7. Terry Eagleton, *Literary Theory: An Introduction* (Minneapolis, 1983), 14; Peggy Bach, "The Searching Voice and Vision of Mary Lee Settle," *Southern Review,* n.s., XX (1984), 846.

8. See Nancy Carol Joyner, "Mary Lee Settle's Connections: Class and Clothes in the Beulah Quintet," *Southern Quarterly,* XXII (1983), 33; Bach, "Searching Voice," 847; and Fanny Butcher, Review of *O Beulah Land,* in *Chicago Sunday Tribune Book Review,* September 9, 1956, p. 2.

is to rely as fully as possible on the spoken language of the represented time, so that *Prisons* is written in the literate, biblically informed voice of a seventeenth-century gentleman, *O Beulah Land* in the harsh voice of the Virginia frontier, *Know Nothing* in a mix of romantic posturing and studied informality characteristic of the antebellum South. Even for readers familiar with the literature of these periods this precision can be daunting, because the spoken language, reconstructed from broadsheets, transcripts, letters, and the like, often seems less regular and recognizable than the language of carefully edited or consciously literary texts. Settle's prose can be trying in other ways as well. Regular syntax and expected constructions are often abandoned, forcing one to enact within individual sentences the process of discovery and reenvisioning demanded in larger ways by the historical narrative as a whole. In one's apprehension of language, as in one's apprehension of the past, too heavy a reliance on habit and formula leads easily to failures in understanding.

Thus Settle's absence of appeal to a sizable popular audience is easily enough explained. However, the difficulties posed by her fiction would seem designed not to discourage but to attract the attention of a critical industry whose primary tasks, at least since the advent of New Criticism, have been to explicate and interpret. Despite the length of her career and the generally respectful reviews, though, Settle has gone so unnoticed by the academic community that the most recurrent subject among those few who have written about her is the fact that she has gone so unnoticed. "Critical response to Settle's work has not reflected her downright awesome accomplishment," according to Nancy Carol Joyner. "Despite positive reactions to her individual volumes, [her] literary reputation remains obscure, and scholarly attention to her work has been conspicuously and mysteriously absent." Bach acknowledges that "Settle's career has been marked by a division in critical recognition and understanding," Jane Gentry Vance that critics have "generally condescended to her historical novels." Garrett, to this point Settle's most ardent supporter, has written that the response to her fiction "can tell us a good deal . . . about the condition of serious criticism in this final quarter of our century."[9] He is correct: not because, as I believe he

9. Joyner, "Mary Lee Settle's Connections," 34; Bach, "Searching Voice," 842; Jane Gentry Vance, "Mary Lee Settle's *The Beulah Quintet:* History Inherited, History Created," *Southern Literary Journal,* XVII (1984), 42; Garrett, "Mary Lee Settle," 281.

means to imply, criticism is today barely capable of recognizing quality, but because the preferences among critics of any age and society tell us a good deal about their "condition," that is, about their attitudes, biases, criteria for judgment, and so on. If one grants that the decision by representatives of a particular culture to accept, or to institutionalize, a writer is at least in part a political and ideological one, then any writer's reputation can be studied in political and ideological terms. Success or failure among the academic critics is no simple question of merit and, though superficially mysterious, can generally be traced to a set of discoverable causes.

Settle, it seems to me, has failed during the past thirty years to appeal to academic critics for several compelling reasons. Vance points to her refusal "to follow fads in fiction writing."[10] I would go further and suggest that she has avoided not only fads but, for the most part, the sorts of consistency in subject, style, and genre that allow writers to be conveniently labeled. Criticism often begins with categorization, and writers who cannot be fitted into a clearly defined category, who belong obviously to no particular area of specialization, tend to be brushed aside in favor of those whose place in the literary hierarchy is more easily assignable. This is not necessarily faddishness or even narrow-mindedness but the inevitable practice of a discipline arranged, in almost every professional and intellectual sense, into distinctly separable fields. To this discipline Settle would naturally seem elusive. She is an American novelist who lived for many years in Europe and whose literary influences seem a mixture of the southern and the continental; she is a writer of novels set in centuries from the seventeenth to the twentieth and in locations from England to West Virginia to Turkey to Hong Kong; her protagonists are male and female, and though her concern with the place of women in American culture is strong, she is not overtly a feminist writer. Students of contemporary fiction are liable to be dismayed by her attention to the past, students of British and American history by her reliance on the formal and stylistic complexities of the moderns. Settle seems so consciously to resist categorization that one wonders if that resistance has become a motivating factor in her work: "You cannot call me a southern novelist; you cannot call me a women's novelist. I like that" (Appendix B, p. 154).

10. Vance, "History Inherited, History Created," 43.

The one category into which Settle has most automatically been placed is, from the point of view of reputation, the least fortunate in many ways. If writing historical novels is a guarantee of mixed reviews, it is an even more certain guarantee of indifference in the academy, which has for most of this century treated historical fiction as a sort of disreputable cousin of the serious novel. Such fiction has long occupied a paradoxical place in the development of and response to the novel, embodying the form at once at its grandest and at its most commonplace. The great historical monoliths at one extreme, *Waverley, Les Misérables, War and Peace,* are countered at the other by the much more numerous historical romances and costume-dramas responsible both for the form's popular success and for its critical disrepute. This disrepute represents an ironic reversal: during much of the nineteenth century, when some of the worst historical fiction in existence was manufactured, the form was nonetheless viewed almost reverently by such writers as Thomas Carlyle, James Fenimore Cooper, Dickens, William Thackeray, and Eliot, who, though only indifferently successful in their attempts at what Eliot called "historical picturing," believed that such picturing seemed "capable of a development that might help the judgement greatly with regard to present and future events."[11] *Romola,* like *A Tale of Two Cities, Henry Esmond,* and a host of other British and American historical novels, may stand as a relative failure precisely because its author was so self-consciously ambitious.

Several developments converged in the late nineteenth and early twentieth centuries to render Eliot's view of historical fiction unfashionable. The general reaction among serious artists against anything characteristically Victorian naturally led to the repudiation of a tradition that had been so enthusiastically embraced by so many canonical authors and to assertions like Arnold Bennett's, in 1903, that the historical novel was an exhausted form. The rise of realism and naturalism, moreover, shifted the focus of novelists increasingly to the contemporary scene, where, as Avrom Fleishman points out, occasional historians such as Ford Madox Ford and George Moore set their "most powerful evocations of social history."[12] The demand for scrupulous accuracy in detail inevitably made representations of the distant past

11. George Eliot, *Essays,* ed. Thomas Pinney (New York, 1963), 446.

12. Arnold Bennett, *How to Become an Author* (London, 1903), 50–51; Avrom Fleishman, *The English Historical Novel* (Baltimore, 1971), 208.

appear unreliable and escapist, and the emphasis, in writers such as Thomas Hardy, on man's helpless participation in historical processes made the less deterministic attitudes of Carlyle or Eliot seem naïve. Modernism's even more radical rejection of both conventional forms and instructive connections to the past intensified further the hostility toward "historical picturing."

Attitudes shaped more than half a century ago still control, at least in part, our response to historical fiction and certainly have affected the critical reaction to Settle. Historical novels continue to be written in large numbers, but even leaving out the very worst, the vast majority descend less clearly from Scott and Cooper than from the popular romances of Edward Bulwer-Lytton and G. P. R. James. The relatively few historical novels taken seriously by critics seem to descend, at another extreme, from books such as Virginia Woolf's *Orlando:* less historical fiction than metafiction, they seem designed to subvert the conventions of the form and to raise questions about the efficacy of literary attempts to reconstruct the elusive past. No longer is the ability of history to "help the judgement greatly with regard to present and future events" accepted as likely or even desirable, and no longer are representations of the past designed scrupulously to exclude signs of the present. John Fowles's *The French Lieutenant's Woman,* Doctorow's *Ragtime,* and even Peter Ackroyd's recent *Hawksmoor* and *Chatterton* have been taken seriously less because they are historical novels than because they are, in effect, fictional meditations on the limitations of narrative history, with the contemporary voice and concerns of the author as prominent as the recreated past. Novels, like those comprising the Beulah quintet, that neither entertain in the manner of the historical romance nor take as their subject their own problematic form are extremely rare and elicit either a confused response or no response at all. One simply has little context in which to judge them.

Historical fiction generally and Settle in particular have suffered during the past few decades from another influential critical preference. The historical novel is perhaps of all fictional forms the one most emphatically insistent on some connection between the imaginary world constructed by the novelist and some larger world existing outside the text: the inclusion of actual historical figures and of details drawn from research into the past represents a belief that the success of the fiction is somehow dependent on its fidelity to life as it was lived. Historical novels, unlike virtually every other literary form, are judged as often in relation to nonfictional narratives and documents as in relation to other fictional texts. For Settle this practice is particularly apt, considering her method of composition. Her own belief that "the work's too hard not to tell the truth, as nearly as you can" (Appendix B, p. 154) has been reflected in her habit of immersing herself, before beginning a novel, in the documents of the past until the verbal habits and frames of reference of an earlier age become part of her contemporary consciousness. It has been reflected as well in the rare critical explorations of her work, which tend to focus on such topics as her use of the voluminous *Thomason Tracts,* a collection of seventeenth-century publications, in writing *Prisons* or her reliance on a five-thousand-page transcript of a Senate investigation into the mine wars in writing *The Scapegoat.* Such source studies, though enlightening and reflective of Settle's own priorities, do little to encourage further discussion. The most influential movements in recent criticism, at least through the 1970s, have been away from an emphasis on the connections between literature and life and thus, in many respects, away from the central aim of historical fiction. If one believes like Wolfgang Iser that the world of fiction is fundamentally "different from the world [the reader] himself is used to," like Roland Barthes that "'characters' . . . can neither be described nor classified in terms of 'persons,'" or like Umberto Eco that even to suggest language "necessarily corresponds to an actual object is a distinctly naive attitude," then the ability of an author convincingly to recreate the past becomes considerably less important.[13] Of course historical fiction can usefully be seen through the eyes of reader-response or structuralist or deconstructive criticism, but those critical approaches tend to erase the identifying characteristics of such fiction and thus to challenge its existence as a definable form. Certainly the traditional emphasis of the historical novelist on "telling the truth" is rendered of less moment or at least is understood in entirely different terms.

13. See Wolfgang Iser, *The Implied Reader: Patterns of Communication in Prose Fiction from Bunyan to Beckett* (Baltimore, 1974), xiii; Roland Barthes, *Image, Music, Text,* trans. Stephen Heath (New York, 1977), 105; and Umberto Eco, *A Theory of Semiotics* (Bloomington, 1976), 61.

It is interesting to speculate about whether the recent emergence of New Historicism, and the consequent redirection of critical attention to the interactions between text and context, will lead to a revival of academic interest in historical fiction. On the one hand, New Historicists have shown no particular inclination to concentrate on the historical novel and have seemed more interested in the historical situations of the writer and reader than in the history represented in the text. On the other hand, New Historicist goals have a great deal in common with goals long articulated by writers of imaginative history. Settle might be defining the New Historicist program when she delineates her intention: "I had to . . . describe not what was happening but what people thought was happening at the time. This was creating their culture" (Appendix B, pp. 162–63). Precisely this attempt at historical and cultural contextualization is at the heart of the contemporary school of historical criticism.

Finally, and in a manner not easy to explain, Settle seems to approach the subjects of family and politics with a passion that appears in its relentless intensity to be strangely alien to contemporary literature. Doctorow, in praising her "sense of the individual as a member of a family and as a political being in history," notes that "there were more writers of this conviction fifty years ago" but "there are precious few now." He is being not necessarily nostalgic or even evaluative but merely accurately descriptive. The truth is that there are very few novelists today who approach their subjects in the manner of Settle and consequently few readers familiar with the sort of world she creates. Earnestness is not a quality one associates with any of the dominant schools of contemporary American fiction; Settle, however, is a profoundly earnest writer who has more than once been likened in "intellectual and moral rigor" to that most earnest of Victorians, George Eliot.[14] Her fiction is consistently informed by a sense of American democracy as "a fascinating revolutionary form of government" (Appendix B, p. 165) and a sense of familial and regional considerations as influences on individual conduct. Whereas these subjects would doubtless have been of concern to George Lewes, F. R. Leavis, and even Lionel Trilling, it is unlikely that they would appeal to the structurally

14. Doctorow, Review of *The Scapegoat,* 1; Bach, "Searching Voice," 849.

and linguistically oriented critics of the past twenty-five years. Settle's conviction, in other words, is not a liability but an irrelevancy. The critical language of an age tends to determine which writers and subjects come most often under critical scrutiny, and contemporary language has had little vocabulary with which to discuss this aspect of Settle's achievement. Her political vision, like her chosen form, happens to occupy one of the few silent spaces in today's noisy analytical discourse.

If the lack of attention paid to Settle is neither a conspiracy nor a sign of bad taste, it is nonetheless a somewhat jolting example of the scarcely noticed power of fashion and expectation to shape the literary canon. In theory her chosen form or theoretical orientation or political idealism should have little to do with the amount, though much to do with the nature, of the critical attention she receives; in practice each has much to do with both. Because there exists no value-neutral or bias-free way of judging literature, this situation is not ultimately correctable: the coming into fashion of Settle's fiction would undoubtedly mean the moving out of fashion of someone else's. The situation is, however, recognizable, and if one can perceive the influence of beliefs and biases on aesthetic judgments, one can perhaps move toward judgments more purely aesthetic. At the very least one can render the question of an author's inclusion in or omission from the canon—until now the question of most concern to Settle's readers—less mysterious and less intrusive. To say that any author should receive more attention is merely to say that the preferences or expectations of an age should be other than what they are.

The reception of the Beulah quintet was not helped by the unorthodox and rather confusing history of its composition. Rather than being able to evaluate a series of novels whose interrelations and controlling structure were relatively apparent, readers were forced continually to reapprehend a series whose shape and dimensions kept changing. If, as is ordinarily the case, the order of publication had corresponded to the order in which the novels were finally arranged, the reaction to the whole would have been less divided, I suspect. Instead, Settle began by writing *O Beulah Land* and *Know Nothing,* eventually the second and third volumes in the sequence and still in many ways the volumes whose connections to one another are most noticeable. These were followed four years later by *Fight Night on a Sweet Saturday,* which was intended initially as the concluding volume of a trilogy but whose relations to the earlier two are less than clear, in part because of some ill-advised editorial tinkering. For *Fight Night* Settle received the worst reviews of her career—even she considers it, in its published form, a failure (Appendix B, p. 161)—and it undoubtedly contributed to a downward revaluation of the earlier historical fiction. Not surprising, her subsequent two books remained firmly in the twentieth century.

The Beulah trilogy continued intact and little read for nearly a decade, until the publication of *Prisons* in 1973. Seventeen years after the appearance of *O Beulah Land,* Settle had now written a novel intended to precede it in the final fictional sequence and to clarify the background and motivations of its central characters. Because *Prisons* was written at what appears, in retrospect, to have been the nadir of Settle's popularity, it received much less attention than it merited and did little to alter the reputation of the previous three novels. Still, the trilogy was now a quartet, with the most recently composed work occupying the earliest place in the fictional chronology. Even seven years later, when *The Scapegoat* turned the quartet into a quintet by fitting between *Know Nothing* and *Fight Night,* the restructuring was not complete. The concluding novel remained a disappointment, so in 1982 Settle reissued it in a dramatically revised form as *The Killing Ground.* Thus the final series, *Prisons, O Beulah Land, Know Nothing, The Scapegoat,* and *The Killing Ground,* took shape over a span of twenty-six years, with each addition demanding that the nature of the total achievement be thoroughly reunderstood. If one grants that each of the novels affects in essential ways one's reading of the others, then the Beulah quintet is, despite its lengthy period of composition, a relatively new work whose final form has only recently become clear. Until now one was reading a work-in-progress.

For the critic of Settle this convoluted history introduces an interpretative complication. In measuring her "downright awesome accomplishment," one has to consider not one fictional structure but two: the final, more obvious structure running from *Prisons* to *The Killing Ground* and the structure, emerging through time, that begins with *O Beulah Land* and *Know Nothing,* detours through *Fight Night on a Sweet*

*Saturday,* and then continues in *Prisons, The Scapegoat,* and *The Killing Ground.* If the novel set in 1912 builds on the one set in 1861, then just as surely the novel written in 1980 builds on the images and ideas of those written during the previous three decades; and if changes in method and design can be expected among novels set centuries apart, then surely they can be expected among novels composed over better than twenty-six years. Does one read *O Beulah Land,* set in 1754, as a continuation of *Prisons,* set in 1649, or *Prisons,* published in 1973, as a follow-up to *O Beulah Land,* published in 1956? To measure these difficulties, one might consider the prospect of interpreting, say, *The Brothers Karamazov* had Parts One and Three been written in the 1870s and Parts Two and Four twenty years earlier, prior to Fyodor Dostoevsky's Siberian imprisonment. Only for criticism that severs all ties between text and context are the complexities introduced not substantial.

One ought to consider as well the peculiar tension that exists among novels designed as both discrete, independent works of fiction and as interdependent segments of a larger literary whole. Settle is emphatic in her insistence that the quintet is not a loosely related *comédie humaine* but "one book" whose parts are inseparable (Appendix B, p. 162). Without the knowledge of humble beginnings provided by *O Beulah Land,* the snobbery of *Know Nothing* would be unironic, and without the latter novel the ancestral connections among the characters in *The Scapegoat* would be undiscoverable. Objects and scenes accumulate and change significance as they reappear from work to work. At the same time, however, too absolute an emphasis on the novels as parts in a whole might lead to the overlooking of some substantial differences. Can the experimental first-person narrative of *Prisons,* for instance, really be considered as belonging to the same book as the more conventional third-person narrative of *O Beulah Land?* Unlike sections of a single long fiction, each of the five novels unfolds an entirely self-sufficient plot, and unlike, for example, Marcel Proust's *A la recherche du temps perdu,* only a handful of minor characters appear in more than one of the works. Although it would be mistaken to read each of the five without knowledge of the others, it might be nearly as mistaken to view them as if they had been published at the same time between a single set of covers.

Ultimately, I think, the novels can best be read and understood in the order in which they were finally arranged (*Prisons, O Beulah Land, Know Nothing, The Scapegoat,* and *The Killing Ground*) and as contributing parts of a single fictional whole. Defining the nature of a discrete book, distinguishing it from a collection of intimately related books, is probably impossible. If the parts of the Beulah quintet are not inseparable, they are at least mutually strengthening, and the strengthening is most dramatic when they are read as a sequence moving chronologically through British and American history. If the differences among some of the novels, particularly those written decades apart, appear distinct, the similarities in theme appear equally distinct and are certainly strong enough to forge an essential connective chain. Finally, if Settle's accomplishment in any one of the novels seems impressive, it is much more so when the five are considered as a lengthy and intricately constructed unit. Because the Beulah quintet was, largely by chance, presented to the world in a manner seemingly designed to minimize appreciation of its virtues, the reader approaching it only now, after its completion, has a peculiar advantage over the reader who encountered the parts as they were published. In effect, the latter has to forget a misleading structure with which the former was never familiar.

The one detail of the quintet's history perhaps most difficult to forget is the thirteen-year separation between the publication of *Know Nothing* and the appearance of *Prisons,* by far the longest gap between any two of the novels in the final sequence. Since this time was not a period of inactivity for Settle—she published three books—it witnessed the sorts of alteration in vision and technique one would expect in a working writer and led to some notable differences between the two novels preceding and the three succeeding it. Settle began as a writer who rendered character and plot primarily through dialogue. By 1953, before she had published a novel, she had written six unproduced plays, and the early *Kiss of Kin* was actually drama revised into fiction.[15] That novel and *The Love Eaters* not only rely heavily on conversation and contain oral imagery in their titles but recall the tight structure, relentless momentum, and irony of tragic theater. Settle has attributed her attraction to the verbal, or avoidance of the visual, to a congenital weakness in eyesight and consequent insecurities (Appendix B, p. 156).

15. Garrett, "Mary Lee Settle," 283.

Equally influential may have been her use of dramatic, conversational novels as models for her own apprentice work. In any case, this emphasis on the spoken exerts a diminished but still noticeable influence on the first two novels in the quintet. *O Beulah Land* and *Know Nothing* may contain a slightly higher percentage of dialogue than do the later novels, but more important, the relationship between the language of conversation and the language of narration is on the whole more conventional: dialogue presents character and the typical voices of the period; narrative, in a distinctly different voice, sets the visual scene. Later, the relations between the two will become more seamless and complex, with the languages of character and of narrator growing closer together and each being used to create a sense of personality and environment. And though even the early novels have moments when the clarity of vision is breathtaking, in the later works these moments become more frequent and more acutely seen.

As one might expect, the early novels are slightly more conventional than the later in a variety of other ways as well. It is probably no accident that *O Beulah Land* and *Know Nothing* are set, respectively, in the pre–Revolutionary War and pre–Civil War years, since these periods are likely to hold a certain amount of intrinsic interest for those even casually familiar with mythologized American history. The settings within which the action of the later novels takes place, for instance, West Virginia during the mine wars of 1912, though possibly of comparable historical moment, are rarely represented in textbooks or in popular fiction and doubtless would seem foreign to all but the most specialized readers. No matter whether the intention be to confirm or to violate them, the novelist ordinarily relies on the existence of expectations of some kind, of established if vague notions about past events, persons, and forms of behavior, in writing historical fiction. That is, the aim is more often to reinforce or revise the sense of a past with which one is already roughly familiar than to introduce a past of which one has absolutely no knowledge. When writing about a relatively unknown age or event, as Settle eventually does, the novelist's job is doubly difficult, requiring not only the revision of historic memory but the creation of memory where none before existed.

One can make comparable distinctions in form. *O Beulah Land* and *Know Nothing,* though never easily accessible, are the most conventionally narrated and arranged of the five volumes. Shifts in point of view and chronology are common enough but for the most part clearly delineated: first-person narration, for example, will be introduced through the familiar device of a letter or journal. Each of the later novels, by contrast, represents a formal departure from convention and from the novels preceding it. *Prisons,* the only first-person narrative in the quintet, is spoken by a character who dies precisely at the close of its final line. Although the action covers only two days, the recollections of the narrator carry the story fifteen years through time, generating sudden shifts in verb tense and chronology, sometimes within a single sentence. Contrasting starkly with the narrative unity of *Prisons* is *The Scapegoat,* the most fragmented of the novels, which gathers together stories told from different perspectives, set in different times and places, into what has been called "a symphony of characters' voices." Joyner has described *The Killing Ground* as "the most experimental of all Settle's books"; it combines the strong central consciousness and free-flowing memory of *Prisons* with the fragmentation of *The Scapegoat* and, as the concluding volume in the quintet, recapitulates voices and images introduced in the previous four.[16] All of the later works seem affected by the postmodern experiments in style and structure conducted by novelists of the 1960s and 1970s.

The unifying consistencies within the quintet, still, are strong enough to overcome such inevitable differences among the volumes. While Settle's methods have evolved over nearly thirty years, her intentions have remained unchanged enough for the pieces of the whole finally to fit together comfortably without extensive revision. The detailed enumeration of these fixed intentions for her work is among the purposes of this book. At the start, however, several might briefly be emphasized, with the aim not of presenting an exhaustive list but of selecting representative examples from a set whose boundaries seem continually to expand as the novels are more carefully studied. Settle appears not to have arrived after the fact at her belief that the novels comprise one book but to have been guided by that belief during the long period of composition.

16. Houston, Review of *The Scapegoat,* 469; Joyner, "Mary Lee Settle's Connections," 42.

Consistency of setting is most apparent. Because the quintet is a study of the genesis of revolution, each novel is situated at a moment when social, economic, and ideological forces are converging to make conflict inevitable. Settle herself has called such moments "pitch points at which the world changes," noting that "there is no way to go back to a world before they happened" (Appendix B, p. 159). Shattuck describes them as lying on the "threshold" of rebellion, Vance as times of "germination, before the seeds blossomed into cataclysmic events."[17] *Prisons* takes place just prior to the period of Oliver Cromwell's dictatorship; *O Beulah Land* builds slowly to 1774, with the pressures that engendered the American Revolution apparent by the story's end; *Know Nothing,* probably most explicit in its foreshadowing of violent conflict, ushers in the Civil War; *The Scapegoat* falls just before the onset of two major developments, World War I and the growth of the American labor movement; and *The Killing Ground,* set from 1960 to 1980, anticipates, then looks back on, the explosion of the civil rights movement and the disillusionment of Vietnam. Because each work is informed by the belief that the great events of history are the predictable, almost mechanical results of processes begun long before and because those events are exhaustively documented and anatomized elsewhere, their direct rendering becomes unnecessary. The recurrence throughout the quintet of these pitch points creates simultaneous impressions of movement and of stasis: the novels carry one rapidly through history, but at each stopping point the same conflicts can be seen as leading inescapably to the same tragic conclusion—a conclusion ironically unforeseen by the actors in the drama but as familiar to the reader as was Oedipus' fate to Sophocles' original audience.

The movement through time is lent stability as well by the continued if altering presence of the land. Aside from *Prisons,* set entirely in England, the novels of the quintet are anchored to the same relatively small stretch of West Virginia territory; and though the action may roam as far afield as London or the Somme, it is always drawn, as if by a magnet, back to the property on the Kanawha River. Again, the effect is a combined awareness of change and changelessness. "The rapid

17. See Roger Shattuck, "A Talk with Mary Lee Settle," *New York Times Book Review,* October 26, 1980, p. 43; and Jane Gentry Vance, "Historical Voices in Mary Lee Settle's *Prisons:* 'Too Far in Freedom,'" *Mississippi Quarterly,* XXXVIII (1985), 393.

transformation of America," suggests William Schafer, is presented in the quintet as one watches the "raw wilderness inhabited by Indians and feral creatures like Jeremiah Catlett . . . transformed into a working farm, a salt mine, finally a coal kingdom."[18] The transformations come not unexpectedly but as outgrowths of seeds carefully planted in earlier novels, as when the salt lick casually mentioned in *O Beulah Land* becomes a prosperous mine in *Know Nothing* or the coal discovered in *Know Nothing* becomes the center of regional life in *The Scapegoat*. Balancing these changes, however, is the sense of permanence created by the continued presence throughout the novels of such recognizable natural landmarks as the river, which as it flows through the quintet virtually takes on the personality of a character, or the shape of the valley itself. Even human additions to the landscape reappear and are reunderstood. When the grave of the murdered con man Squire Raglan that was dug in *O Beulah Land* is romanticized in *Know Nothing* into an Indian burial mound, the sense of timelessness created by the invulnerability of the grave itself seems inseparable from the sense of evolution created by its misinterpretation. Like many imaginative historians of the nineteenth century, Settle uses the sheer physical presence of the land to place in perspective the changes wrought by time and man.

This balance between stasis and change is reinforced by the passage through three centuries of language itself. One of the distinguishing features of the quintet, noted earlier, is Settle's attempt to write each novel, as nearly as possible, in the spoken language of its time, so that the reader moving in order from *Prisons* to *The Killing Ground* in effect receives a fragmentary lesson in the history of English. The development of any language is evidence of both the ability of ideas to survive through time and the power of time to shape and modify ideas: for every word whose meaning continues for centuries unchanged, there is another whose meaning alters with the altered understanding of each new age. Thus the quintet allows us to witness, on the one hand, the carrying of Johnny Church's seventeenth-century idioms into the discourse of the twentieth century and, on the other, his richly biblical language transformed by each generation into something altogether

18. William J. Schafer, "Mary Lee Settle's Beulah Quintet: History Darkly, Through a Single-Lens Reflex," *Appalachian Journal*, X (1982), 85.

different. The continuity of names operates in a similar way. Whereas it is striking that the same set of names recur in characters born centuries apart, it is equally striking that "Catlett," a name signifying poverty in the eighteenth century, signifies wealth in the nineteenth or that "McKarkle" is the name of very minor characters in the first few novels but of the protagonist in the last.

The aim of this multivolumed exploration of the past is, simply, to tell the truth. This claim seems ridiculously commonplace, like saying that language is important to a poet or that the difference between appearance and reality is a prominent literary theme. But the urge to tell the truth, not just to be lifelike but to be true to life, is as powerful in the Beulah quintet as in any work of contemporary fiction and shapes the formation of each text on virtually every level. It serves, for instance, as a principle of selection: unlike many writers of historical fiction, who will take liberties with dates, places, and persons for dramatic or formal purposes, Settle feels absolutely bound by events as they appear to have happened. The novelist can extrapolate from the facts, naturally, and can superimpose on them the most elaborate fictional inventions but can no more responsibly ignore the facts than can the social historian. From names mentioned briefly in a seventeenth-century bulletin, she can fashion the complex characters of Johnny Church and Thankful Perkins; but if those characters encounter Cromwell at Naseby, it must be at a moment when Cromwell is known to have been at Naseby. The difference between the historical novelist and the historian, in Settle's view, is not that the novelist is free to alter the facts but that through the imaginative devices of fiction she is empowered to look at the facts in a different light.

Truth becomes not just subject but theme in each of the novels, for as the truth is pursued, the elusive nature of truth itself is explored. One is reminded throughout the quintet that personal memory, limited by prejudice, desire, and forgetfulness, is often an unreliable means of recovering the past. Perhaps more important is the reminder that communal memory, the sense of the past possessed by a family or even a culture, may be equally unreliable, deformed by the shared dreams of a community the way personal memory is deformed by the dreams of an individual. Each novel is antimythological, a stripping away of the invented layers that distort and obscure the truth, and inasmuch as the setting is largely southern, the myths exploded are primarily those of the South. Because in all the novels but the first the reader has a more immediate knowledge of the past than do the characters, he is usually in a position to gauge the difference between actuality and recollection: each time a murderous mercenary is transformed by a subsequent generation into a hero, each time a dirt-poor background is remembered as aristocratic ancestry, the causes and extent of the distortion can be determined. There is no more compelling reason to read the novels in sequence.

The incessant search for truth dictates even the structure of individual novels. Since personal memory and memories shared within homogeneous groups can be faulty, the best way to discover the nature of past events is to draw upon the recollections of as many different people with as many different viewpoints as possible. Stories told from a single point of view, even one relatively honest and enlightened, are liable to be untrustworthy, so most of Settle's fiction relies on shifts in focus, person, and verb tense to introduce a variety of perspectives into the narrative process. In *The Scapegoat,* where truth is most clearly understood as an amalgam of different points of view, the narrative fragmentation is most radical; in *The Killing Ground* the voice varies from first to third person and, within the first dozen pages alone, the verb tense from past to present to future. The first two novels remain more conventionally in the third person, but because the central character in each shifts repeatedly, the consciousness through which the narrative is filtered frequently changes. *Prisons,* exceptional in many ways within the quintet, is the only novel spoken throughout from the same first-person viewpoint, though even there diversity is introduced through the fluctuation between past and present perspectives and through the speech of characters representing a wide range of beliefs. For the most part, one approaches truth in these narratives obliquely, glimpsing fragments of it in the pictures individual characters present and gathering those fragments together to form a picture more nearly, though never entirely, objective.

Fiction so infused with an awareness of bias and self-interest as determinants of behavior might easily become harshly contemptuous of its subject. Settle's is the opposite. Her recognition of universal human failings leads not to condemnation but to widespread empathy. If within each being is a flaw meriting criticism, within each as well is a virtue meriting praise or at least a depth of suffering deserving compassion. Among the reasons her fiction provokes so complex a response is her refusal to make predictable moral judgments about any of her characters. There may be a few legitimate heroes throughout the five volumes, but there are no absolute villains because there are no characters whose actions are seen without some measure of sympathy. Unifying the quintet, in other words, is a generosity of spirit that allows Cromwell, ideologically the enemy in *Prisons,* to be seen more in sadness than in anger and the petty cruelties of Sally Lacey in *O Beulah Land* to be mourned rather than reviled. Here, again, Settle recalls George Eliot, of all novelists the one most devoted to the broadening of the reader's moral imagination. "But why," her narrator asks in *Middlemarch,* "always Dorothea?" The perspective of the sympathetic observer is more comprehensive:

> Was her point of view the only possible one with regard to this marriage? I protest against all our interest, all our effort at understanding being given to the young skins that look blooming in spite of trouble; for these too will get faded, and will know the older and more eating griefs which we are helping to neglect. In spite of the blinking eyes and white moles objectionable to Celia, and the want of muscular curve which was morally painful to Sir James, Mr. Casaubon had an intense consciousness within him, and was spiritually a-hungered like the rest of us.[19]

Because we recoil automatically from Casaubon as from comparable characters in the Beulah quintet, Eliot and Settle labor, sometimes to the point of overintrusiveness, to weaken the influence of conventional expectations on our sympathies. "You can't write down characters without having a strong empathy for them," Settle has insisted. "A person is dead on the page if you do" (Appendix B, p. 158).

Universal sympathy leads in Settle as in Eliot to the clarity of vision required of the reader if he is to perceive the strong but easily overlooked web of relations connecting individuals wholly unaware of their presence. "The inspiring principle which alone gives me courage to write," claimed Eliot, "is, that of so presenting our human life as to help my readers in getting a clearer conception and a more active admiration of those vital elements which bind men together." Garrett

19. George Eliot, *Middlemarch* (1871; rpr. New York, 1977), 192.

writes similarly of Settle's fiction, where continually "discoveries are made" and "relationships, kinships of people, and of events, are established."[20] The families introduced in *O Beulah Land,* the Catletts, Laceys, Brandons, McKarkles, Cutwrights, and Kreggs, interweave throughout the subsequent novels, as in a geometric expansion of the inbreeding in *Wuthering Heights,* until the original strands are virtually impossible to disentangle. And as in Settle's best-known nonhistorical novel, these "blood ties" become merely representative examples of a wide range of likenesses binding apparently disparate people and events together. Since characters are only rarely reduced to one or two dominant traits and only rarely denied authorial empathy, their similarities are more apparent than would otherwise be the case. Where in most fiction the sympathetic side of the villain or repellent side of the hero might be excluded, here they are more likely to be included and seen, unexpectedly, to overlap.

Many of the distinguishing qualities identified to this point can be seen as well in Settle's nonhistorical fiction. The virtual obsession with truth, the effort to empathize and to uncover connections, even the attraction to especially meaningful moments in time, more or less characterize everything she has written. The Beulah quintet is set apart and provided its most impressive unity by the idea of history, and of meaningful historical re-creation, that runs through all five volumes. What chiefly distinguishes the quintet from the dozens of historical novels manufactured yearly is what distinguishes all lasting from ephemeral historical fiction: an interest in the movements and implications of history itself, in what Fleishman calls "human life conceived as historical life," as opposed to an interest merely in a particular historical period.[21] Because human beings are seen always as participants in a process stretching backward and forward through time, the ways in which they are affected by that process and, more rarely, may in turn affect it are incessantly examined within and among the novels. Freedom and control, desire and responsibility, and impulse and law become only some of the opposed terms in a complex network of tensions shaping personal, familial, and national life. Emerging from this long examination

20. George Eliot to Clifford Allbutt, August, 1868, in Eliot, *Middlemarch,* 594; Garrett, "Mary Lee Settle," 287.

21. Fleishman, *English Historical Novel,* 11.

is nothing less than a theory of the relations between the individual will and external forces in history.

Here, finally, is where the originality of the Beulah quintet must be discovered. Writing an important historical novel, let alone a series of related novels, means not only confronting the intricacies of history but bearing the burden of a complex, self-referential, insistently didactic tradition of historical fiction reaching back nearly two centuries. Few would feel the anxiety of influence more strongly than would the novelist writing historical fiction in a manner descending from Scott, Eliot, and Tolstoy. Settle manages to combine a thorough familiarity with the tradition from which she emerges with an original vision of the past. Put another way, she adapts a tradition largely European and conservative to subjects American and revolutionary. For whereas historical fiction of this depth and extensiveness had been written before, never had it been written by an American author attempting to define the characteristically American historical experience. Although the nature of the result must always be arguable, the attempt, really the only one of its kind, is undoubtedly to seek in the past the meaning of *being* American—of being formed by a peculiar set of social and historical pressures, as Tolstoy had sought the meaning of being Russian—and to discover, as Settle has written, "the birthright earned by nameless people through the 300 years of our becoming."[22]

22. Mary Lee Settle, "Recapturing the Past in Fiction," *New York Times Book Review*, February 12, 1984, p. 37.

# History in Fiction 2

Among the reasons for modern critical wariness of the historical novel is surely the elusiveness of its definition. Virtually all fiction, by virtue of its verb tense, takes place prior to the moment of its telling and is in that sense a re-creation of "history," so the identification of characteristics that distinguish the specifically historical novel becomes problematic. Simply drawing a line, back a generation or fifty years or prior to the author's lifetime, beyond which the setting of a novel becomes historical is convenient but arbitrary. Besides, no matter where the line is drawn, one is left with the problem of how to categorize the many novels whose action begins and ends on opposite sides of it. Too general a definition ("a historical novel is a novel the action of which is laid in an earlier time," or "historical fiction is fiction in which history is important") may be all-encompassing but is critically useless; a definition too restrictive or theoretically sophisticated may exclude the majority of popular novels most readers consider historical.[1] The reviews of Settle's novels have already illustrated what confusions may arise when dissimilar works are grouped automatically under the same ill-defined heading.

If historical fiction tends at one extreme to become indistinguishable from plain fiction, it tends at the other to become indistinguishable

1. Ernest E. Leisy, *The American Historical Novel* (Norman, 1950), 5; Monroe K. Spears, *American Ambitions: Selected Essays on Literary and Cultural Themes* (Baltimore, 1987), 199.

from plain narrative history. From almost the moment of the novel's creation, back to *The History of the Adventures of Joseph Andrews* and beyond, workers in the form have struggled to differentiate their aims and strategies from those of historians, recognizing at once that any simple differentiation between truth and untruth would be inadequate and epistemologically weighted against the activities of the novelist. The notion that fiction writers bring to the facts a greater degree of freedom, creativity, or shaping imagination, popular in the nineteenth century, has been called into question in the twentieth, as historiographers from R. G. Collingwood to Hayden White have pointed to the narrative historian's inevitable reliance on those creative, even fictive activities traditionally assigned to the novelist. "So far from relying on an authority other than himself," Collingwood wrote in 1946, "the historian is his own authority and his thought autonomous, self-authorizing, possessed of a criterion to which his so-called authorities must conform and by reference to which they are criticized." White notes that recent critiques of narrative discourse by historiographers coincide with "the rejection of narrativity in literary modernism and with the perception, general in our time, that real life can never be truthfully represented as having the kind of formal coherency met with in the conventional, well-made, or fabulistic story." In the relatively recent past, he continues, "it was possible to believe that whereas writers of fiction invented everything in their narratives—characters, events, plots, motifs, themes, atmosphere, and so on—historians invented nothing but certain rhetorical flourishes or poetic effects to the end of engaging their readers' attention and sustaining their interest in the true story they had to tell."[2]

Undermining this belief now is our sense of the relativity of historical truth and, perhaps more important, our recognition that the narrative form is itself a means not merely of organizing but of imposing meaning: storytelling presupposes the "adequacy of stories" to represent "the reality whose meaning they purport to reveal."[3] Possibly because, as Dominick LaCapra suggests, "the kinds of narrative employed by historians have tended to remain rather conventional," less reflexive

2. R. G. Collingwood, *The Idea of History* (New York, 1946), 236; Hayden White, *The Content of the Form: Narrative Discourse and Historical Representation* (Baltimore, 1987), ix, x.

3. White, *Content of the Form,* x.

and self-referential than those employed by novelists, their fictive and rhetorical strategies have gone relatively unnoticed.[4] Critics such as White and LaCapra hesitate to classify as purely fictional or as purely historical not only obvious hybrids, *In Cold Blood* or *The Executioner's Song,* for example, but also any narrative that claims to represent reality and to assign a meaningful order to events, that is, any narrative at all.

Rather than attempt precisely to define and delimit a genre so diverse in quality and intention, it seems practical to grant that historical novels comprise an immense, varied, and only roughly definable group, what LaCapra calls a "hybridized genre," but that within this group one can identify a tradition of works, written by serious novelists, that share subjects, themes, and attitudes. It is this tradition, not historical fiction in its broadest sense, about which most critics of the genre have written and concerning which they appear to have reached reasonable unanimity of opinion. When Georg Lukács wrote that historical novels were shaped by a view of existence "as something historically conditioned" and of history as a force "which deeply affects . . . daily lives," he was, of course, referring not to "blowzy Technicolored so-called historical romances" but to the fiction of Scott, Cooper, and Honoré de Balzac.[5] His argument that the distinguishing characteristic of historical fiction is the perception of history as a dynamic process impinging on the present, not to mention his prescription for the most veracious manner of representing past events, remains the foundation upon which most subsequent definitions of the form have been constructed. "What makes a historical novel historical," Avrom Fleishman has since claimed, "is the active presence of a concept of history as a shaping force." Harry Shaw has suggested that the best historical novels convey "the recognition that human beings are part of a larger historical process" that affects their existence "through specific and unique social mediations"; recent critics, including Philip Fisher, Barbara Foley, and George Dekker, have begun their work with comparable assumptions.[6] It would not be an exaggeration to suggest that Lukács has played a

4. Dominick LaCapra, *History, Politics, and the Novel* (Ithaca, 1988), 8.

5. *Ibid.,* 6; Georg Lukács, *The Historical Novel,* trans. Hannah Mitchell and Stanley Mitchell (Boston, 1962), 24.

6. See Fleishman, *English Historical Novel,* 15, and Harry E. Shaw, *The Forms of Historical Fiction: Sir Walter Scott and His Successors* (Ithaca, 1983), 25–26.

role for twentieth-century critics of historical fiction analogous to the role Scott played for nineteenth-century writers of historical fiction. Each established a conceptual model largely, if not wholly, accepted by his successors. Contemporary critics all nod to Lukács and agree that what makes fiction historical in the most important sense is the use of history not as setting but as subject: the location of the action in a carefully rendered period in the past is not an end in itself but a means of revealing with special clarity historical processes at work. Such a definition of historical fiction allows not only for the exclusion of the majority of popular costume-dramas but for the inclusion of novels set only shortly before the time of their composition, as when Fleishman includes *Tess of the d'Urbervilles* because it is about the effects of history or Settle includes *The Killing Ground* even though its action ends virtually in the present.

The historical fiction with which I will be concerned, then, is usually, but not always, set in an age prior to the author's own and takes as one of its central subjects the effects of the historical process on individual and social life. Although the life depicted may be that of the past, the life implicitly the object of study is almost always contemporary. History is explored as a guide not to vanished predecessors who are past caring but to those alive at the current moment. What Jerome McGann argues about historical criticism, that is, appears equally true of traditional historical fiction: the "focus upon history as constituted in what we call 'the past' only achieves its . . . fulfillment when that study of the past reveals its significance in and for the present and the future." Prior to the nineteenth century such fiction could not exist, since, as Foley points out, "it is only in the nineteenth century that the term 'history' comes to denote not merely a mode of discourse or a universal process of change, but a crucial context for understanding the present." The most influential (and impenetrable) definer of this shift in meaning has been Michel Foucault, who calls the nineteenth century the Age of History and locates there the initial use of history "to deploy, in a temporal series, the analogues that connect distinct organic structures to one another."[7]

7. McGann, *Beauty of Inflections,* 25; Barbara Foley, *Telling the Truth: The Theory and Practice of Documentary Fiction* (Ithaca, 1986), 144; Michel Foucault, *The Order of Things: An Archeology of the Human Sciences* (New York, 1970), 219.

Because historical fiction arose in this environment not as an isolated phenomenon but as one literary manifestation of newly understood relations between past and present, only with difficulty can one separate its growth from the growth and popularity of a variety of other genres, including the histories of Carlyle and Thomas Macaulay, the social panoramas of Balzac, the huge, backward-looking poems of Alexander Pushkin, Alfred, Lord Tennyson, and Robert Browning, the art histories of John Ruskin and Walter Pater, even, I believe, the scientific studies of Charles Lyell and Charles Darwin. Only with difficulty can one distinguish between the rise of the historical novel and a number of more general developments in the form of the novel itself. The eighteenth-century emphasis on relatively static characterization shifted, increasingly as the subsequent century wore on, toward a reliance on evolving characters shaped by personal history, to the extent that the career of and the altering critical response to a dominant novelist like Dickens reveal fundamental changes in theoretic assumptions. Moreover, physical settings, once roughly sketched, became precisely localized and subject to changes as dramatic as those within characters. The rise of the *Bildungsroman,* the novel of development, reflects as clearly as does the rise of the historical novel an interest in comprehending the present in terms of the past.

Out of this interest grew a European fictional tradition of common emphases, themes, even rhetorical strategies (distinct, for reasons I shall pursue, from much of the historical fiction written in America). Its settings tend to be historical periods, and its subjects historical events, comparable in important ways to the present, so that what Carlyle calls the "ever-growing fabric" connecting moments in time can be laid bare. The opening of *A Tale of Two Cities,* emphatically juxtaposing Victorian England and an earlier period ominously "like the present period," typifies the dual focus of the age's imaginative histories. Seldom have writers of a particular form tried so consciously to react to, modify, and even mimic the work of their predecessors, and seldom, consequently, has a literary tradition proven to be so clearly defined and self-referential. Within a remarkably short time, Walter Scott became as influential a forebear for writers of historical fiction as Homer had been for writers of epic, and virtually every major English, French, German, and Russian novelist of the time tried his or her hand at the form Scott was understood to have originated. "It was Sir Walter Scott," notes Dekker, "who created both the genre as we know it and an immense international market for more books like *Rob Roy* and *Ivanhoe*."[8]

Nineteenth-century imaginative history, particularly in England, is distinguished by its formal diversity and ideological consistency. Works as dissimilar in subject and style as *The Stones of Venice* and *Barnaby Rudge* or *Past and Present* and *The Ring and the Book* share explicit assumptions about the importance and preferred uses of history and the most reliable methods of historical re-creation, as well as implicit assumptions about the likelihood and desirability of certain kinds of social and political change. George Eliot, writing in the 1870s as this homogeneous tradition was already breaking apart, describes in her notebooks the view of "historic imagination" that had dominated the previous three decades:

> The exercise of a veracious imagination in historical picturing seems to be capable of a development that might help the judgement greatly with regard to present and future events. By veracious imagination, I mean the working out in detail of the various steps by which a political or social change was reached, using all extant evidence and supplying deficiencies by careful analogical creation. How triumphant opinions originally spread—how institutions arose—what were the conditions of great inventions, discoveries, or theoretic conceptions—what circumstances affecting individual lots are attendant on the decay of long-established systems,—all these grand elements of history require the illumination of special imaginative treatment. . . . I want something different from the abstract treatment which belongs to grave history . . . and something different from the schemed picturesqueness of ordinary historical fiction. I want brief, severely conscientious reproductions, in their concrete incidents, of pregnant movements in the past.

One cannot but be reminded of Eliot's claim in 1855 that "there is hardly a superior or active mind of this generation that has not been modified by Carlyle's writings," since the model of historical narrative she constructs here is in substance, if not in rhetoric, Carlylean.[9] Carlyle's German-influenced essays of the 1830s—"On History," published

8. Thomas Carlyle, "On History Again," in *Selected Essays* (New York, 1972), 98; Charles Dickens, *A Tale of Two Cities* (1859; rpr. New York, 1973), 35; George Dekker, *The American Historical Romance* (New York, 1987), 1.

9. Eliot, *Essays,* 446–47, 212.

in 1830, "Biography," in 1832, and "On History Again," in 1833—together with Scott's novels, form the basis for the theory and practice of imaginative history through much of the nineteenth century and, arguably, through much of the twentieth as well. The central principles articulated by Carlyle and invoked by Eliot are clear enough:

One, the writing of history is extremely, perhaps uniquely important. For Carlyle it is not merely the "fittest study" of modern times but "the only study" that "includes all others whatsoever."[10]

Two, this writing, in its most advanced and inspired form, should be neither completely factual nor completely imaginary but somehow should combine verifiable facts ("extant evidence") with the artist's shaping vision ("careful analogical creation").

Three, facts chosen for illumination should range in scale from the most mundane to the most extraordinary, and characters from the meek to the mighty, bringing together in historical writing a familiarity with common life and an awareness of the power of special moments and individuals to transcend and forever reshape the common.

Four, imaginative re-creation of history should draw from it some moral, psychological, or spiritual meaning that expands beyond the specific historical moment and applies as well to other places and times. Understanding history, that is, should allow us to see in the past the seeds of the present and future and to witness the moment "pregnant movements" conceive current events.

Five, only the exceptional individual, sometimes called "heroic," sometimes "artistic," is gifted with what Ruskin calls "the far sight . . . that separate[s] man from man, and near[s] him to his Maker," that is, the ability to see within his or her own time the transcendent, ahistorical meaning.[11]

Obviously Carlyle, Eliot, and the rest prescribe the form, texture, and intellectual aims of what one might consider mainstream narrative history, fictional or nonfictional. Less obviously they reveal a number of beliefs about the nature of the historical process and about the kinds of social and political change such a process should, ideally, bring about. As much as history shapes the way these writers view the world,

10. Carlyle, "On History Again," 91.

11. John Ruskin, *The Seven Lamps of Architecture* (1848; rpr. New York, 1974), 176.

their view of the world shapes the way they understand history. Little is random or incoherent about the movements of history as imagined by the major Victorians. Its messages are readable by the educated eye and, by implication, written in a rule-governed, learnable, though admittedly elusive language. Its movements are ultimately controllable or at least predictable, hence the usefulness of studying history at all. The same faith directs the historian as directs the preacher or the teller of morally instructive tales—the faith that judgment is improvable and that "present and future events" may therefore be handled more wisely than comparable events in the past.

Although there is some variation in political and social vision among major nineteenth-century works of history and historical fiction, most are shaped, explicitly or implicitly, by what Foley terms a "complacent conservatism."[12] That this vision predominates seems not only unsurprising but ideologically inevitable. The impetus behind the rise of imaginative history was the desire to establish illuminating connections to the past, to carry the best of the past into the present, and certainly to avoid abrupt disjunctions between successive generations. The obsessive focusing on moments of revolutionary conflict reflects not so much a need to understand revolution as a desire to avoid revolution's recurrence and, particularly in Scott, Dickens, Thackeray, and their imitators, to depict the subsuming of radical extremes into a moderate, stable, and distinctly bourgeois present. Books such as *The Heart of Mid-Lothian,* Dekker correctly observes, were written for "a society which rejects revolution but accepts gradual change" and, I would add, by authors sharing those sentiments. If the historical process is understood as gradual and progressive, then the writer's "now" must be understood as both founded on and better than the recent past. Future change, potentially more judiciously carried out because based on a knowledge of history, should be neither too rapid nor too dramatic. When the present is criticized, as in the more nostalgic works of Carlyle and Ruskin, it is for abandoning wholly the values of the past; when the future is envisioned, as at the end of *A Tale of Two Cities,* it is as a continuation of a balanced present (minus the more obvious evils). Pos-

12. Foley, *Telling the Truth,* 177. For the best discussions of this subject, see Foley, *Telling the Truth,* 153–77, and Robert Clark, *History, Ideology, and Myth in American Fiction, 1823–52* (London, 1984), 45–46.

sibly the central message of this historical tradition is that revolutions are "inevitably disastrous."[13]

American contemporaries of Scott and Dickens were cognizant of, but did not wholly share, this widespread European interest in historical re-creation. Certainly they elected not to enshrine history as the "fittest of all subjects" or to follow with any consistency the theoretical model outlined above. The classic explanation for this difference in interest has been that of Henry James, who asserted in his study of Nathaniel Hawthorne's works that American writers simply did not move in a culture with "an accumulation of history and custom . . . a complexity of manners and types" sufficient to generate a profound interest in its own past.[14] In effect, he suggested, no rich past existed for an American novelist to draw on. James, writing in 1879, was less originating an argument than carrying forward one that had been voiced by American novelists for more than a half-century. Hawthorne himself, in his Preface to *The Marble Faun,* complained that "no author, without trial, can conceive of the difficulty of writing a romance about a country where there is no shadow, no antiquity, no mystery, no picturesque and gloomy wrong, nor anything but a commonplace prosperity." Even Cooper, the nearest American equivalent to the Europeans, conceded that "there is no other country, whose history is so little adapted to practical illustration as that of the United States of America."[15]

Although the claims of James and the rest have some merit, they should be seen as revealing less an absence of history than an absence of desire to represent it. Surely America had a history in the broadest sense, that is, an event-filled and partially documented past not entirely unlike the British past recorded in the novels of Scott. Why American writers chose not to categorize this past as historical or to assign it a central place in their fiction is easy enough to discover. For Americans of the nineteenth century, a decisive artistic break with the past seemed not only permissible but preferable or even necessary. "The nineteenth-century American," writes Harry Henderson, "would never be able

13. Dekker, *American Historical Romance,* 9; Nicholas Rance, *The Historical Novel and Popular Politics in Nineteenth-Century England* (London, 1975), 19.

14. Henry James, *Theory of Fiction,* ed. James E. Miller, Jr. (Lincoln, 1972), 49.

15. See Nathaniel Hawthorne, *The Marble Faun* (1860; rpr. Columbus, 1962), 3. Cooper's remark, from his 1832 Preface to *Lionel Cooper,* is quoted in Clark, *History, Ideology, and Myth,* 166.

simply to accept history as an extension of the present into the past." To do so would be to erase the distinctions between the New World and the Old, to diminish the uniqueness of American experience and minimize its separation from European experience, frustrating what Monroe Spears calls the "fundamental [American] ambition . . . to break with the past and with the Europe that embodies it."[16] Democracy, at least in theory, is designed to free the individual from many of the constraints of history so powerful in cultures long dominated by aristocracies. The antirevolutionary stance of British writers in particular, implicit, as I suggested, in the historical form itself, was to a large degree inconsistent with America's vision of itself as a new civilization founded on the death of an older one. Whereas for Scott and Dickens, therefore, a historical analogue to the present was enlightening, for most American novelists of the time it was liable to seem reactionary, even authoritarian.

Recently critics including Robert Clark and Philip Fisher have pointed to a more covert, less ennobling reason for the nineteenth-century American avoidance of history. "The primary quarrel of American history," Fisher suggests, "is the ever-shifting battle between white settlers and Indians over the white claims to the land that they found already peopled by the Indians." Accurate historical representation, by depicting the realities of colonization and conquest, would have come into conflict with America's idealized image of itself, rendering problematic any claims about freedom or Manifest Destiny. The real "threat of historical objectivity" was that it might reveal either inconsistencies between Americans' rhetoric and their behavior or underlying similarities between American and European uses of power.[17] It was thus better to dismiss history as limiting or old-fashioned and, once one was freed from the requirements of truth, imaginatively to transform the past into a harbinger of the nation America was destined to become. If the expressed European desire was to read the future in the details of the re-created past, the (unexpressed) American one was to re-create the past out of the details of a determinate future.

Nineteenth-century American historical fiction therefore does not

16. Harry B. Henderson III, *Versions of the Past: The Historical Imagination in American Fiction* (New York, 1974), 6; Spears, *American Ambitions,* ix.

17. Philip Fisher, *Hard Facts: Setting and Form in the American Novel* (New York, 1985), 53; Clark, *History, Ideology, and Myth,* 46.

take the direction of European: its preeminent examples form not a reasonably unified genre but a series of distinct works bearing relatively little relation to one another. There is no clear tendency to set historical novels in critical periods comparable to the present, nor is there any overt awareness within the novels themselves of earlier works of historical fiction. In his study of the historical imagination in American fiction, Henderson considers, among others, the Leatherstocking Tales, *The Scarlet Letter, Billy Budd, Foretopman, A Connecticut Yankee in King Arthur's Court,* and *The Red Badge of Courage*. Most noticeable when one compares this list to a contemporaneous British list, including, say, *Old Mortality, A Tale of Two Cities, Henry Esmond, Romola,* and *The Trumpet Major,* is the much greater diversity of intention and achievement represented by the American works, along with the comparable absence of a distinct, unifying tradition. *The Scarlet Letter* and *A Connecticut Yankee* are similarly historical only in the technical sense that both are set clearly in the past. One might select any two novels from the British list and discover far more substantial thematic, stylistic, and formal resemblances. Twain's well-known dislike of both Scott and Cooper exemplified at its extreme the inclination of many American historical novelists to dissociate themselves from their predecessors.

While there is no definable tradition to which these American works of historical fiction belong, there seem at least to be shared tendencies distinguishing them from works in the European tradition—tendencies toward what might be called the mythic and the epic. Claude Lévi-Strauss draws a distinction between historic and mythic representation, noting that though "a myth always refers to events alleged to have taken place long ago," it derives its "operational value" from the timelessness of the pattern it describes.[18] Mythic events, in other words, derive no special meaning from being situated at a particular historical moment. Hayden White, going further, writes that "mythic narrative is under no obligation to keep the two orders of events, real and imaginary, distinct from one another," recalling Hawthorne's admission in "The Custom House" to taking "nearly or altogether as much license as if the facts had been entirely of my own invention" and Emerson's attempt "to

18. Claude Lévi-Strauss, *Structural Anthropology,* trans. Claire Jacobson and Brooke Grundfest Schoepf (New York, 1963), 209.

make the historical sense entirely subjective."[19] The separation between extant evidence and analogical creation, so important to the British, holds no power over writers unconcerned with conforming to documented truth. Protagonists such as Natty Bumppo, Hester Prynne, Billy Budd, and Huckleberry Finn, moreover, resemble the immense heroes of epic more than they do the lower-case heroes of conventional historical fiction. "When Cooper reincarnates the heroes of Homer, Milton, and the Bible in the New York wilderness," Dekker writes, "when Hawthorne recalls the Gray Champion to life, or when Edith Wharton makes us see Helen of Troy in Ellen Olenska, they are doing what the authors of literary epic have always done." These are not the rather translucent, passive characters whose thinness, Harry Shaw notes, allows "historical processes to shine through more clearly" but relatively changeless figures struggling against historical inevitability. The heroes of epic, Lukács argues, are "the national heroes of a poetic view of life," the heroes of historical fiction "of a prosaic one." American historical fiction has been in this sense more "poetic" than European fiction has been. Again, Avrom Fleishman distinguishes between epic poetry, which, as defined by Aristotle, tells how "a person of a certain type will on occasion speak or act," and historical fiction, which addresses "a specific past situation in all its concreteness."[20] American historical fiction has been more concerned with the actions of "a person of a certain type" than with the presentation of a specific, concretely realized past. The historical setting functions to separate the hero from familiar man by locating him in the past and to authenticate him through association with actual events and cultures. However, these events and cultures are seldom presented in much detail, certainly without the wealth of detail in which Scott presents the Highland uprisings or Tolstoy Napoleon's invasion of Russia. For Edward Waverley and Pierre Bezukhov to have full meaning, they must be seen as shaped at least partially by actual moments in history. Billy Budd's meaning no more depends on the reality of the events of 1797 than does Achilles' on the events of the Trojan War.

19. See White, *Content of the Form,* 3–4; Nathaniel Hawthorne, *The Scarlet Letter* (1850; rpr. Columbus, 1962), 33; and Clark, *History, Ideology, and Myth,* 47.

20. Dekker, *American Historical Romance,* 59; Shaw, *Forms of Historical Fiction,* 48–49; Lukács, *Historical Novel,* 38; Fleishman, *English Historical Novel,* 8.

Two examples might help to underscore these important differences in approach. Cooper is the American novelist most often linked to the European tradition generally and to Scott specifically. His differences from Scott, however, are instructive. Although Lukács likens Natty Bumppo to the typical hero of Scott's fiction, the two embody noticeably different types. The hero of a Scott novel is, as Lukács admits, "always more or less mediocre"; Natty Bumppo, as a soldier and as a moral force, is not.[21] Scott's heroes are torn between opposing historical forces, classically between allegiance to an aristocratic heritage and attraction to the ideals and glory of a rebellion. Their struggle with and resolution of the conflict dramatize for Scott the historical process at work. Natty Bumppo is not torn. His allegiances are absolute, and his struggle is not to mitigate between opposing, equally attractive extremes but to maintain his position despite the onslaught of historical change. Scott's heroes are thoroughly enmeshed in history; Natty Bumppo is above it, resistant to it. They typify man at a particular historical moment; he is a type.

Melville's *Israel Potter: His Fifty Years of Exile,* published in 1854 and considered his most overtly historical work of fiction, seems also to be modeled on European antecedents. Like *Barnaby Rudge* and *Henry Esmond,* the novel focuses on a period of violent conflict; like *Past and Present* it relies heavily—too heavily some have said—on documentary and narrative sources; like *Waverley* it takes as its hero a historically representative man and includes among its characters actual historical figures, including Benjamin Franklin and John Paul Jones. Melville mimics the European tradition, however, not to exalt but to belittle it. Progress in this bleak novel is illusory, attempts to control external events fruitless, and the sure determination of historical truth impossible. In one way or another, Melville suggests, all re-creations of history become the creation of myth. While retelling the story of America's rebellion against Britain, the narrative becomes itself a wry rebellion against the confident, restrictive, and largely conservative beliefs of British historical literature.

For reasons touched on in the previous chapter, neither the European nor the American historical novel has in this century been granted

21. Lukács, *Historical Novel,* 33.

privileged status or been written with notable frequency. However, among American novelists particularly, one can isolate two primary directions in which the interest in the relations between historical fact and imaginative creation has been channeled. As novelists have become even "less willing to make assumptions about what 'reality' is," about where one draws the line between fantasy and truth, they have tended to move toward one of two opposite extremes: either the overtly mythic, fantastic, and idiosyncratic or the insistently matter-of-fact and reportorial. At a loss for how to distinguish between history and fiction, in other words, they have opted to write historical fiction that either openly proclaims or utterly disguises its fictionality. Writers who subordinate fact "to a mythic or highly personal view of history" and who grow naturally out of the nineteenth-century mythic tradition include Faulkner, John Barth, John Hawkes, Doctorow, and Thomas Pynchon. Writers at the other extreme, including John Dos Passos, Norman Mailer, James Baldwin, and Truman Capote, "have tended to opt for a far narrower canvas, taking a small slice of historical reality and endowing it with 'plot' and significance."[22] These "non-fiction novelists," to borrow Capote's phrase, have moved toward a more faithful and exhaustive representation of historical actuality than nineteenth-century novelists would have sanctioned, and they have consciously shunned the interpretation of historical process and the juxtaposition of past and present of which their predecessors were so fond. The message emerging from these two artistic camps seems to be that either one fictionalizes and interprets history by wholly subjugating it to the writer's will or one records it, journalistically, with as much accuracy and as little imaginary embellishment as possible. If the middle ground—in the nineteenth century the novelist's high ground—has not vanished, its size has diminished significantly.

Understanding the background and varied uses of historical fiction allows for the contextualizing and appreciation of Mary Lee Settle's somewhat paradoxical achievement. If one keeps in mind that the beliefs and methods of classic historical fiction have rarely been brought

22. John Hollowell, *Fact and Fiction: The New Journalism and the Nonfiction Novel* (Chapel Hill, 1977), 9; Barbara Foley, "From *U.S.A.* to *Ragtime:* Notes on the Forms of Historical Consciousness in Modern Fiction," *American Literature,* L (1978), 101.

to bear on American experience, that these methods have almost always been used in the service of a conservative ideology, and that many novelists in this century have called into question the viability of historical fiction itself, then the quintet must appear, at the same time, both unusually responsive to tradition and unusually resistant to the pressures of expectation and convention. Few important works in contemporary literature are so without immediate predecessors and successors, yet few are so overtly conscious of assuming a place in an extensive and complex genealogy. That is, the originality of the Beulah quintet consists not in any absolute severing of connections but in the re-creation of a nineteenth-century European conservative tradition from a twentieth-century American revolutionary perspective. This re-creation is more than a mere technical curiosity: Settle manages more successfully than writers of either flamboyantly mythic or insistently journalistic historical fiction (between whom, I think, she might be placed on a continuum running from pure fantasy to pure fact) to express a philosophy of history, to place individual events in American history into a larger context, and to define an idea of the characteristically American experience. Because the methods of Scott and Tolstoy, in her view, successfully uncover the roots of a culture, she borrows them; because American culture is different from British or Russian, she rethinks and adapts them.

Personal and cultural circumstances have combined to create in Settle a writer prepared to empathize with the situation of nineteenth-century historical novelists. The pull of order, custom, and tradition identified by James as missing from American life seems nearly as strong within Settle's southern culture as within the older cultures of Europe. A woman raised in this culture, expected to conform to a variety of restrictive models, seems particularly likely to feel both the comfortable allure and tyrannical demands of the past, that is, to be caught in a position very like the one dramatized in the most influential historical novels. Because she lived for a long period in Europe, moreover, Settle "began to write with a European sensibility" (Appendix B, pp. 153–54) and was able to combine even in her earliest fiction elements of southern and English traditions. She has been as well suited to Europeanize the American historical novel as was James, for different reasons, to have a comparable effect on the American novel of manners.

The definition of imaginative history drawn earlier from the essays of Eliot and Carlyle serves almost as a blueprint for the historical fiction of Settle. Her belief in the importance of historical re-creation is nearly Carlylean in its intensity, and the terms in which she has for years defended her chosen form recall the ideology and images used by the major Victorians. Historical novels, she has written, satisfy an urge to discover personal identity "that cannot be satisfied by the more disciplined and defined study of history." She concludes: "It is only through fiction that we can learn something real about individual experience. Any other approach is bound to be general and abstract."[23] Fiction written without any awareness of historical truth, at the other extreme, is likely to reinforce "false memory" (Appendix B, p. 156) and to tell us even less about ourselves than the most impersonal histories. The attempt to locate truly imaginative history between these poles is precisely the task George Eliot is about when she calls for "something different from the abstract treatment which belongs to grave history" and "from the schemed picturesqueness of ordinary historical fiction."

What Roger Shattuck says about Settle's work, that "investigative research and the imagination work hand in hand" in her novels, is true but possibly misleading: her fiction is no dramatization of research notes. Imagination, in her view, does not simply extrapolate from or build upon a solid foundation of verifiable fact but gives shape and significance to facts that would otherwise be formless and silent. The historical truth at the heart of the quintet she seems to perceive as a kind of rough ore, potentially revealing but meaningless without the processing carried out by the artistic imagination. "*O Beulah Land*," she has written, "was there in fragments to be unearthed and transmuted into fiction." The roots of this idea can be traced, again, to the nineteenth century and the rise of the belief, as Collingwood states, that "the part played by the historical imagination . . . is properly not ornamental but structural," and thus without that imagination "the historian would have no narrative to adorn." Such a belief informs the work not only of such historians as Carlyle, Macaulay, and Ruskin or of such novelists as Scott and Eliot but of a poet such as Browning, whose *The Ring and the Book* is one of the representative products of

23. Settle, "Recapturing the Past," 1. For the last two sentences of this remark, Settle is indebted to the Italian critic Nicola Chiaromonte.

the Victorian historical imagination. In language similar to Settle's, Browning describes how his "fancy has informed, transpierced" the "pure, crude fact" and how he has "fused [his] soul with that inert stuff" to produce "prime nature with an added artistry," the "one way possible of speaking truth."[24] So far as I can tell, there is no important difference between Browning's sense of fusion or transpiercing and, more than a century later, Settle's of transmutation: in both cases imagination is seen not merely as a means of filling in gaps in historical record or of making history entertaining but as the only available way of bringing life and relevance to inert factual material.

Any distinction between truth and imagination is liable to seem artificial at a moment when both the fictiveness of "grave history" and the truthfulness of imaginative extrapolations are prominent topics of discussion. Settle insists on such a distinction, however, as a means of avoiding historical relativism and the mythologizing that is characteristic of both American historical fiction and the cultural memory of the American South. This is not to say that she perceives truth as simple or easily apprehended: as I suggested in Chapter One, the core of truth in her novels is often an amalgam of differing points of view, none of which grasps the truth of events in anything near its entirety. The power of historical fiction is precisely its ability to bring together these various partial perspectives so that the reader can arrive at an understanding more comprehensive than that of any of the participants in the historical events. Blurring the distinction between history and myth leaves one with only some individual's or culture's version of what the past might have been—a version in which massacres might become victories or acts of cowardice feats of heroism. "Myth," Settle has said, "can be psychically true, and at the same time it can be a cover-up for the past." And when myth is simply untrue, when it becomes "a mixture of nostalgia and forgetting," it can be dangerous (Appendix B, pp. 160, 159).

Like many earlier historical novelists, Settle believes that only by exploring all levels of society and all manner of events can one reveal the true meaning and form of the past. The Beulah quintet includes, at one extreme, several major battles, several overtly momentous confron-

24. Shattuck, Introduction, xiv; Settle, "Recapturing the Past," 36; Collingwood, *Idea of History,* 241; Robert Browning, *The Ring and the Book* (1868–69; rpr. New York, 1961), 1–2, 11, 477.

tations, and such figures of historical stature as Cromwell and Mother Jones. But because Settle wants to write "not simply of what happened, but of what people thought was happening at the time," her primary emphasis is on "commoners instead of kings, incidents instead of panoramas or great events." Here she might be paraphrasing Lukács in his definition of the classic historical novel. "What matters," he writes, "is that we should re-experience the social and human motives which led men to think, feel, and act just as they did in historical reality." For the exploration of these motives "the smaller . . . relationships are better suited than the great monumental dramas of world history." Lukács, in turn, might be elaborating on Carlyle: "He who sees no world but that of courts and camps, and writes only how soldiers were drilled and shot, and how this ministerial conjurer out-conjured that other, and then guided, or at least held, something which he called the rudder of Government . . . will pass for a more or less instructive Gazetteer, but will no longer be called a Historian."[25] One of the ways historical novelists have from the start distinguished their activities from those of conventional historians is by proclaiming their ability to shift the focus of the narrative, through the exercise of imagination, from the great man who lived to the humble one who might have.

Each volume of the quintet is meant to have what Lukács identifies particularly in Scott as a "felt relationship to the present." Settle claims, "I chose, throughout the Beulah quintet, those neglected times that combined the seeds of cataclysm and change, before the impossible had become possible and the unthinkable, historic fact." This concern with tracing "how the seed was planted and how it grew" recalls the generative metaphor of Eliot, whose interest as a historical novelist was in representing "pregnant movements in the past." Pregnant movements, which give birth to subsequent events and ideas that bear importantly on the present and future, are the focal points of this group of novels in which history is imagined as an endless "series of beginnings."[26] Each work, as I earlier noted, ends on the brink of a major conflict.

25. Settle, "Recapturing the Past," 36–37; Lukács, *Historical Novel,* 42; Thomas Carlyle, "On History," in *Selected Essays,* 87.

26. Lukács, *Historical Novel,* 53; Settle, "Recapturing the Past," 36; Shattuck, "Talk with Settle," 43; George Garrett, "Mary Lee Settle's Beulah Land Trilogy," in *Rediscoveries,* ed. David Madden (New York, 1971), 175.

Watching repeatedly the inexorable movement toward explosive events and becoming sensitized to the implications of even minor attitudes and actions, one is made aware by analogy of the connections between the represented past and the lived present and, inevitably, between the present and the future. Like *Prisons'* Johnny Church, we recognize that "already there [is] a new pattern if we could [see] it," but we are "so blinded . . . that most of us [see] it not" (114).[27]

Those able to see even dimly the unfolding pattern, those gifted with Ruskin's "far sight," become the heroes in Settle's historical drama. At rare, climactic moments, Shattuck writes, "a perceptive individual may participate fully in a recognizable event of genuine significance to him and to others." Developing the ability to participate knowledgeably in events, to perceive the historical significance of the present, became in the nineteenth century the primary reason for the writing and reading of history: the implicit hope was that through study of the past many could acquire the visionary power possessed inherently by the heroic few. This hope was easily turned into yet another argument for the preeminence of the historical novel. The artist, blessed presumably with this special vision, was better able than the mere scholar to illuminate history through, in Eliot's words, "special imaginative treatment." Settle's belief in the novelist's ability to satisfy deeper urges than the historian can reach, to hear in the past echoes "more profound and more elusive," may be her most powerful inheritance from the nineteenth century.[28]

Moving through this sort of ideological checklist is a clear, if slightly artificial, way of demonstrating Settle's reliance on a nineteenth-century European sense of history and of historical fiction. Upon that foundation one can begin to build a precise understanding of how she adapts and alters these conventional ideas. The central dilemma in her fiction—the dilemma she sees as unavoidably, and in some ways uniquely, American—is between obedience and rebellion, between respect for manners and order and structure on the one hand and a powerful urge for freedom and self-determination on the other. Suspended between

27. All page references to novels by Mary Lee Settle, unless otherwise specified, are to the editions published by Scribner's in the Signature series (New York, 1987–88). Page references will hereinafter be given in the text.

28. Shattuck, Introduction, xvi; Settle, "Recapturing the Past," 1.

these two extremes, pulled powerfully toward both, are most individuals in America and, to a degree, the whole American democratic system. The dilemma of the individual is articulated by the strong-willed and alienated narrator of *The Clam Shell:*

> I sense for a second the point of poise where I will have to live, between dry pastlessness, where only the mind functions and no one is born and no one dies, and that singing insistence of the blood I share with them to leave the self unformed, bitter, hopeless, and child-like in service to others who have done the same. I know the blood will call, accuse, and try to drown me, and out of fear of loneliness I will yearn for the comfort of sweet defeat, its unquestioning protected dead calm. . . . It is a kind of death I envy with my whole tentative soul, that certainty, that limbo, that ease. (172–73)

This "point of poise" is Settle's area of concern in every novel. Balanced on one side is "that singing insistence of the blood," that urge to be "child-like in service" to family, community, and culture. Her fiction is densely populated with imposing parental figures who require just such homage. The urge is seductive in its invitation for one to seek guidance and certainty and to avoid the lonely terrors of freedom; it is particularly strong, in Settle's view, in a country so obsessed with responsibility to family as America. "There's an awful prisonlike fraud that I think we create very strongly in this country," she has said. "Maybe we have to be so dependent on family because we don't have much communal sense, especially with the huge immigrations that clutch together" (Appendix B, p. 164). Balanced on the other side is "dry pastlessness, where only the mind functions," in other words, the less comfortable but equally insistent impulse to sever connections and to act according to beliefs and desires of one's own. This impulse, too, Settle sees as particularly strong in America, where individualism has always been championed in rhetoric and law. In all her novels characters are caught between these opposing lures, sometimes moving, after a struggle, toward one extreme but never losing entirely an awareness of the other.

In her historical fiction Settle attempts to place this struggle into a larger context and to show how it has been inherent in American experience and systems from the beginning. Each novel in the quintet dramatizes an archetypal conflict between forces of control, which must by definition be present in any system of government, and demands for freedom, which must just as inescapably be present in the system created in America. The frontier wars of *O Beulah Land,* the Civil War of *Know Nothing,* and the mine wars of *The Scapegoat* embody the divided nature of the land where Uncle Sam and Brother Jonathan, figures of paternal guidance and fraternal equality, competed for representative status, or where fatherly presidents are challenged endlessly by a "legislative band of brothers" (Appendix B, p. 165). As *Prisons* is intended to demonstrate, little else could be expected from an order founded by a gathering of "dis-orderly" rebels.

Settle's interest in these warring forces is entirely consistent with her interest in traditional historical fiction; indeed, it may be the best way to account for her longstanding, and from a practical standpoint untimely, attention to the form. Like Settle's, Walter Scott's novels were designed, and his protagonists selected, to highlight the strength and moral ambiguity of the conflict between responsibility and freedom, or between the need to maintain order and the need to bring about beneficial change. As early as 1820, Samuel Taylor Coleridge identified in Scott a "contest between two great moving Principles of social Humanity": between "religious adherence to the Past and the Ancient" on the one hand and "the mighty Instincts of Progression and Free-agency" on the other.[29] Virtually all of Scott's successors take up the identical problem. Almost without exception, however, and in a manner very unlike Settle's, the forces of conflict in these novels are ultimately resolved into a familial, social, and political structure based on moderation and compromise. The conflict, in the end, is shown to be a temporary, if potentially recurrent, historical phenomenon. For example, at the conclusion of *Barnaby Rudge* one learns that "it was a very long time before Joe [Willet] looked five years older, or Dolly either, or the locksmith either, or his wife either," and at the end of *Henry Esmond,* that "the drama of [Esmond's] life was ended" and replaced by "immense happiness . . . for so many years."[30] Behind the rhetoric of the conventional happy ending is a sense of conflict, or drama, giving way to tranquility, time to timelessness, change to permanence. The tumult

29. Samuel Taylor Coleridge, *Collected Letters,* ed. E. L. Griggs (6 vols.; Oxford, 1971), V, 34–35.

30. See Charles Dickens, *Barnaby Rudge* (1841; rpr. New York, 1973), 735, and William Makepeace Thackeray, *Henry Esmond* (1852; rpr. New York, 1970), 512.

that formed the subject of the novel is perceived finally as a state of disequilibrium from which the central characters have thankfully and irrevocably emerged.

Tension, in Settle, is the only American equilibrium. The struggle between responsibility and freedom is unresolved because it is unresolvable. Movement through history, rather than carrying one beyond conflict, carries one perpetually between a fixed pair of oppositional pressures, and the strong characters are those who can withstand them without retreating to the safety of blind obedience. In this more frightening world, the equivalents of Edward Waverley can look forward to no cessation of turmoil, because there will always be demands made from without and resistance to them generated from within. Thus, no novel in the Beulah quintet ends in the sense that the pattern it dramatizes reaches completion: the narratives stop, but often at a moment when conflict and uncertainty are most intense. The protagonist-narrator of *Prisons* asks, on the novel's last page, nine unanswered questions; the heroines of *The Scapegoat* and *The Killing Ground* set off on journeys whose destinations are difficult to predict; and the hero of *Know Nothing,* the story situated at the center of the quintet, remains momentarily frozen at the heart of a storm:

> As in other moments in his life, he knew complete stillness, the stillness of the woods, of sorrow, of night—just for a moment, acting on him. He knew it had begun and the luxury of questioning was over, thrown away. He had not said a prayer alone since he was a child. He knelt by the window, his hands clutching the window ledge.
>
> "Oh God," he prayed, "forgive us our sins and don't let me have to kill my brother."
>
> After he had gone to try to stop the running retreating mob, there were only the marks of his fingers left white on the dirty sill. (334)

Here again is that "complete stillness," that point of poise between beckoning extremes. Unlike the stillness at the conclusion of *Barnaby Rudge* or *Henry Esmond,* this one carries no promise of happiness and seems to deny, even in the ephemeral dust on the sill, the possibility of permanence or certainty.

"Hovering over all Settle's work," Peggy Bach suggests, "is the atmosphere of the Greek tragedies." Certainly this interpretation is true if one sees that tragic atmosphere charged by the painful and neverending tension between necessity and free will. In this sense most nineteenth-century historical fiction is decidedly untragic, though the conflicts these works describe often carry the potential for tragedy. (Once more, Melville's *Israel Potter* stands as an American criticism of a European model; one of the few works of historical fiction informed by a tragic vision, it ends with the protagonist utterly "repulsed in efforts" and "faded out of memory.") Settle herself has emphasized particularly the relevance of the Antigone myth to the dilemma in her fiction. "The model is Antigone," she has said, "for all the principal characters" in the quintet. "The oscillation between Antigone and Creon . . . gives movement to all the volumes."[31] Creon embodies national interest, historical necessity, and all the other forces that work against the assertion of freedom; Antigone stands as the apparently powerless figure who is free nonetheless. The focus is on oscillation: this struggle in Settle tends not toward the utter triumph of either antagonist, though one may win temporarily, but toward an almost symbiotic balance. She analyzes the relationship in this way: "It took a long time for me to realize that Antigone and Creon need each other, that the balance point is between them. So neither one of them is right, and neither one is wrong. It's the tension between them that makes for a democratic system. If Creon wins, it's dictatorship; if Antigone wins, it's anarchy" (Appendix B, pp. 164–65). If Creon wins, one might add, it's tragedy; if Antigone wins, it's epic or even comedy. Settle locates her historical fiction, as well as the characteristic American experience, at the moment, present in virtually all narrative literature, just before it becomes clear whether events are tending toward a tragic or toward a comic resolution.

Although Antigone and Creon need each other, Settle herself is constitutionally "more akin to Antigone than to Creon," and her fiction focuses more on the forces of rebellion than on the forces of control. Again, this situation is nothing entirely new. From Bonnie Prince Charlie to Lord George Gordon to Savonarola, the doomed rebels have been the most charismatic figures in conventional historical fiction. The primary difference is that these earlier outlaws are in the end perceived

31. Bach, "Searching Voice," 848; Herman Melville, *Israel Potter: His Fifty Years of Exile* (1854; rpr. Evanston, 1982), 169; Shattuck, "Talk with Settle," 44.

as unrealistic, misguided, or anachronistic failures, while Settle's characters, who believe themselves failures, can be seen from the reader's perspective as having shaped the course of history. Bonnie Prince Charlie believes himself to be controlling history but is not; Settle's typical rebel believes himself not to be controlling history but is. What emerges, in effect, is an anti-great-man, and thus, in some ways, an anti-nineteenth-century, theory of history. "One of the themes of the [quintet]," Settle has said, "is that we know more about the past than the people who were living in it knew when it was the present" (Appendix B, p. 162). The characters in her novels who claim to comprehend fully the historical implications of the present (Cromwell in *Prisons,* the slave owners in *Know Nothing*) are generally proven wrong, whereas those who confess ignorance or are burdened by a sense of failure often appear successful or even visionary as the quintet evolves. One of the ways she democratizes historical fiction is by granting to every character she creates, much more openly than her predecessors do, the power to cause historical change. In Settle's world, as Joyce Coyne Dyer notes, "civil wars arise not from isolated events or decisions of kings and great men, but, rather, from anger, outrage, and tension within individuals and families."[32] Characters trapped in almost every observable way are yet free to alter the shape of the future.

No work of European and few works of American historical fiction are so intent as the Beulah quintet on exploring the roots and implications of freedom. The tone of this exploration is neither complacent nor self-congratulatory: for every characteristically American assertion of freedom, there has been an equally characteristic attempt at repression; for every benefit conferred by living in a relatively free society, there has been a substantial price exacted. The tension between benefit and price, in fact, becomes the subject of every novel, as the narrator of *The Killing Ground* recognizes on the quintet's final page: "I knew that I had joined the wanderers . . . all of those who have set out alone, perhaps self-deluded by necessity. But it was the wanderers who had given us a country, and left the scars behind. Deep within us there had been instilled an itch, a discontent, an unfulfilled promise, perpetually

32. Settle, "Recapturing the Past," 37; Joyce Coyne Dyer, "Mary Lee Settle's *Prisons:* Taproots History," *Southern Literary Journal,* XVII (1984), 29.

demanding that it be kept. Johnny and Thankful, and all of us, would always fail and always win, and eternal vigilance and our sense of loss, of being unblessed, were the price of freedom" (384). Uncertainty and ambivalence, obviously, mark even this climactic moment of insight. The reconciliation with paternal authority that ends the traditional historical novel does not come here, because it cannot come. America, in Settle's view, was founded and continues to be refounded on the denial of such reconciliation. Whether the rewards of freedom are substantial enough to justify the consequent sense of loss, of being "unblessed," is a question asked, and variously answered, by every major character in the work.

One of my intentions in discussing the individual novels in the quintet is to trace the recurrence of these central conflicts and questions and thereby to suggest the coherence of the multivolume work as it was finally arranged. The reader's understanding of the issues at stake deepens as the later novels repeat and amplify the patterns begun in the earlier. *Prisons,* the foundation on which the entire sequence is constructed, dramatizes the most overt conflict between authority and freedom, in effect introducing and defining the terms necessary for the informed reading of the subsequent novels. It is the briefest and most concentrated novel of the five, and its protagonist, Johnny Church, the most unambiguously heroic character. *O Beulah Land* and *Know Nothing,* the two most intimately linked works in the quintet, transfer the English conflict of *Prisons* to America and show the opposed forces persisting even as they grow less easily distinguishable. Although the story they tell is relatively self-contained, for these novels were written more than a decade before any of the others, its historical inevitability is underscored by the English preface. *The Scapegoat* and *The Killing Ground* redefine the conflict in modern and increasingly female terms and present an even more complicated set of personal and social dilemmas. The last novel in particular, self-consciously allusive to the earlier ones, is likely to appear shapeless when seen as an independent work. Because acts of assertion and concession carried out in a New York apartment tend to be quieter and more internal than those occurring on the American frontier, their significance is easily missed if one reads them without an awareness of the past from which they emerge. *The Killing Ground,* like all that is ill-defined in contemporary life, is contextualized and clarified by history.

# *Prisons* The Unblessings of Our Fathers 3

*Prisons* is at once the marginal and the central novel in the Beulah quintet, standing apart from the others in subject and style yet developing more explicitly than they the images and ideas that unify and structure the long historical narrative. None of the other novels is told entirely in the first person or set entirely in England or organized so tightly around a single central character. Largely absent are the fluid perspective and chronological fragmentation characteristic of Settle, along with, to a lesser degree, the limitless extension of moral sympathy. More decisively, perhaps, than in any of her other novels, heroes and villains here are identified, defined, and judged. *Prisons* recreates the most famous historical figure and most dramatic series of historical events in the quintet, incorporates the most material taken verbatim from documentary sources, and relies most explicitly on established literary models. It is the briefest of the novels and the one marked by the most powerful sense of closure. Even the publication history of the quintet sets *Prisons* apart. At the beginning, separated by four years, come *O Beulah Land* and *Know Nothing;* at the end, separated by two years, come *The Scapegoat* and *The Killing Ground. Prisons* sits isolated in the center, published in 1973, thirteen years after its predecessor and seven years prior to its successor.

Rather than weakening the connections between *Prisons* and its successors, however, these peculiarities point to the special importance of its introductory role. Like an expository opening act or a symphonic overture, it remains separate from but essential to all that follows, a concentrated prefiguring of things to come. If the through-running subject of the quintet is, as I have suggested, the inevitable democratic tension between freedom and authority, then *Prisons* defines and dramatizes that tension most precisely. And because the terms of the conflict are at the start relatively straightforward and unambiguous, one can trace them the more easily through the fragmentary, multilayered narratives that follow. Johnny Church, *Prisons'* narrator-hero, is literally and figuratively the progenitor of a huge cast of later characters and is recalled, sometimes explicitly and sometimes in brief hints, by every other protagonist in the sequence. The novel's many recurrent images—images of flowing water, vegetation, and especially, of course, prisons—will reappear throughout the quintet, as will the Creon-Antigone myth that *Prisons* self-consciously invokes. Even the relations between historical movements and the individual will are explored more thoroughly in this novel than in any of the others.

There is another paradox: despite the fact that *Prisons* appears in time and place furthest removed from Settle's personal history, it is the novel in the quintet most reflective of her own nature and of the era in which it was composed. She describes its genesis in this way: "Of all the volumes, the most truly autobiographical, the most urged on me by present circumstance, was *Prisons*. It was conceived in 1968 when this country succumbed to the backlash that elected Richard Nixon. I saw the antiwar marchers whipped in Chicago by the police. In the same month in Prague the young and spirited were beaten into submission by the Soviet Army. Out of fear, and a hope that blasted hopes survive the hopeful, I found *Prisons* and Johnny Church. I am Johnny Church." Subsequently she has alluded to *Prisons* as her *David Copperfield* (Appendix B, p. 151), as a favorite among favorites and a recasting into fictional form of intensely personal impulses and dilemmas. Not surprising, given this authorial endorsement, the novel has attracted more critical attention than any of her others, with a number of readers echoing George Garrett's view that it represents "a great leap forward, a kind of 'breakthrough' from a steadily built canon of excellent fiction to . . . something more."[1] The addition of *Prisons* to the original Beulah

1. Settle, "Recapturing the Past," 37; Garrett, *Dictionary of Literary Biography,* 284.

trilogy, nine years after its "completion," was the first and probably the most important of several steps that reshaped and substantially improved the overall work and was in effect the beginning of Settle's more mature reconsideration of her own earlier concerns.

The novel's general subject is the complex web of political conflicts among the competing factions during the English Civil War and particularly the conflict between Cromwell, an embodiment here of intransigent authority, and the Levellers, the radically democratic wing of the Parliamentary army. To a much greater degree than Parliament, which represented primarily the interests of the gentry, the New Model Army in general and the Levellers in particular, an offshoot of the army named probably for its advocacy of the leveling of various social and political class distinctions, represented the concerns of the population as a whole. "Historians now generally accept," notes Jane Gentry Vance, "that from 1646 the Levellers were a third force (along with Parliament and military leaders) that influenced Cromwell to take more democratic positions than he might otherwise have taken."[2] Eventually Cromwell grew impatient with the Levellers' resistance to his demands, especially their refusal to go to Ireland to subdue the Catholics, and in 1649, after three years of escalating tension, he executed some of their leaders, co-opted others, and frightened many of their followers into submission. Still, Settle suggests, the Levellers contributed directly through emigration and indirectly through the articulation of democratic principles to the conception of freedom that subsequently formed the United States.

To dwell too exhaustively on the precise details of this confrontation would be misleading, however, since its rendering in the novel is, by comparison to most works of narrative history, fragmentary and abbreviated.[3] Rather than being given the panoramic, footnote-laden perspectives of Scott or Tolstoy, one is presented through the first-person narrative of Johnny Church with "history . . . in fits and starts, glimpses, chunks of events seen from queer kaleidoscopic angles."[4] The

2. Vance, "Historical Voices," 397.

3. The best summary of the historical events on which *Prisons* is based and of the documentary records through which Settle learned of those events is provided by Vance in "Historical Voices." Of primary importance are the *Thomason Tracts,* "a collection of Civil War pamphlets, newspapers, and communiques that contain contemporary accounts of the executions" of Johnny Church and Thankful Perkins (*ibid.,* 395–96).

4. Schafer, "History Darkly," 80.

historic importance of men such as John Lilburne, of places such as Naseby and Burford, is less explained than assumed. Settle's inclusion of an explanatory foreword and afterword points to the absence within *Prisons* itself of enough information to piece together anything like a complete history of the period. The action of the novel, centered on the crisis of the Cromwell-Leveller conflict in May of 1649, is an extrapolation from, but not an enactment of, documentary history; the mass of evidence that contributed to her formation of the action has little place within a compressed, stylized narrative that is designed less to proclaim its own truth than to draw meaning from the peculiarly archetypal and influential series of events she is dealing with.

Settle wastes little time in announcing, and the word is suitably emphatic, both the nature of *Prisons'* narrative voice and the extent of the novel's stylistic separation from conventional historical fiction:

> I am twenty today. There is only Thankful Perkins to tell it to, but Thankful is asleep. He has that soldier's way of catching sleep when he can. His head is bowed on his tarnished beaten iron breast and jogs in rhythm with his horse. His pot has fell over his eyes. His hands rest on the pummel and move on their own like little animals or when a child sleeps and its hands go on playing in a dream. How small he is. He looks fourteen, and lost in this great flat valley of the Thames. Who would know, watching him ride along there with his mouth fell ajar, that he is as fine a soldier as I have ever known and so compassionate and loving a friend? Why, he can speak with the tongues of angels, and he has, shining sometimes in his dirty face, the wonder of one newborn every day. (15)

Most of what one needs to know about the style of *Prisons* is explicitly or implicitly revealed in its opening paragraph. That the novel's initial two words ("I am") manage to establish both the first person and the present tense surely is no accident. Relatively few historical novels are told in the first person, and in those few that are, the speaker tends to be a marginal rather than a central character—a character who observes almost in the manner of a third-person narrator—or to incorporate into his story enough letters, speeches, and similar paraphernalia to broaden the narrative perspective. An interesting exception is Marguerite Yourcenar's *Memoirs of Hadrian,* published in 1951, a first-person narrative spoken by the Roman emperor and one of the modern historical novels most admired by Settle. Because Hadrian is so centrally placed, however, and because he is panoramically surveying his life and times from the vantage point of his deathbed, his narrative provides the scope and sweeping interpretation characteristic of the historical novel.

The reasons for the tendency of historical fiction to broaden the narrative perspective are clear enough and underlie some of the harsher criticism of *Prisons*. William Schafer, for example, complains that as a consequence of the first-person voice "the large interpretive role of the historical novelist is atrophied, and we are fettered to limited, often monochromatic narrative perspectives," and Kathleen Swaim, looking for the history in this historical fiction, is frustrated by the "blindered perspective of an individual participant in a numerous host."[5] Historical fiction, these criticisms imply, is expected to be panoramic, to balance individual experience against an awareness of broad movements, and to eavesdrop on pivotal decisions and confrontations. Managing all this within the monologue of a single, historically inconsequential actor in a larger drama is virtually impossible. Unlike Tolstoy, free to move from Prince Andrei to Pierre or from battlefield to drawing room, Settle remains trapped within the perspective of Johnny Church, while historically significant events unfold elsewhere.

Comprehensive history is sacrificed, to a greater degree in *Prisons* than in any of the other novels, because the establishment of a distinctive voice and gradually evolving consciousness for Johnny Church is crucial. More than any other character in the quintet, Church must be fully and sympathetically rendered since through his decisions and experiences the idea of heroism informing all five novels is defined. Among the traditional strengths of first-person storytelling is its tendency to render all but the most reprehensible characters sympathetic and familiar, and among the benefits of so extensive a monologue is the likelihood that the personality of its speaker will remain memorable enough to be recalled through four subsequent volumes. The danger here is that the novelist will create a voice so sympathetic and comfortable that the sense of historical unfamiliarity, of different ages producing different modes of consciousness, will diminish and the presentation lapse into what Schafer calls "ahistoricity."[6] This Settle combats through the subtle but pervasive strangeness of Church's language. The

5. Schafer, "History Darkly," 80; Kathleen M. Swaim, "A Fictional Gloss on the History of the 1640's," *Milton Quarterly,* XV (1981), 98.

6. Garrett, *Understanding Mary Lee Settle,* 45; Schafer, "History Darkly," 81.

seventeenth-century grammatical constructions ("His pot has fell" and "with his mouth fell ajar"), the biblical imagery ("he can speak with the tongues of angels"), and the poetic cadences mark the speaker as someone who not only speaks differently but forms ideas and likenesses differently than does the contemporary reader. That Church's language is historically true—that his saying "you" instead of "thee" puts him "in one particular social and educational category" (Appendix B, p. 164) or that his speech patterns are modeled skillfully on the tracts and broadsheets of the time—is probably less immediately important than its mere difference, its oddness. Gradually, as one begins to learn why Johnny Church speaks as he does and how his speech shapes and is shaped by his ideas, its historical fidelity becomes a means of understanding his seventeenth-century mind.

More daring was the decision to write the story in the present tense or, rather, to write it in the voice of a character who dies at its conclusion, since, barring the supernatural, that decision necessitates a present-tense narrative. Aside from accommodating the death of Johnny Church, however, the present tense offers a number of technical and cognitive advantages. Placing the events of the novel's present into the present tense helps clarify the time frame of a narrative in which flashbacks are frequent and sometimes abruptly introduced and in which the distinctions between actions and the memories they evoke are often blurred. Occasionally it is only the shift in verb tense that reveals the shift from description to recollection. As in the *nouveau roman,* moreover, identified by Settle as an important contemporary influence (Appendix B, p. 152), the present tense alters the way one apprehends the novel's events, lessening the separation between the experiences of character and reader and minimizing, or disguising, the interpretive role of the author. Thus, in the complex interplay between distance and intimacy that must characterize the reader's response to any historical novel, the verb form works to balance the estrangement generated by the seventeenth-century language and ideas.

The novel's "now" is a three-day period in May of 1649 during which Johnny Church and Thankful Perkins move from the "great flat valley of the Thames" to the town of Burford, where, victims of Cromwell's crushing of Leveller resistance, they are apprehended, tried, and executed. Threaded throughout the narrative are Church's recollections of events covering fifteen years and culminating in his present circumstances. He was raised under the guidance of a puritanical father who had worked and married his way from a chandler's shop into the gentry. Because Church's time as a child was divided between his own austere household and Lacy House, the more lavish and free-spirited estate of Sir Valentine, his maternal uncle, his strongest memories seem to be of polar oppositions: of demands for allegiance from father and uncle, of conflicting ideas of courtesy and grace, of dimly understood "tugs-of-war between kings and parliaments" (35). Values appear relative and therefore, to the child, uncertain. Hovering over these earliest scenes is Church's sense of being insignificant and unformed during the period "when we are small and those who rule over us are too tall for us to see their eyes" (16). His linked feelings of powerlessness and guilt—"[my father] rose so high above me that I thought I had done wrong" (40)—recall, perhaps deliberately, Pip shrinking from the Pumblechookian elbow or Copperfield from Mr. Murdstone's glare.

Dramatized repeatedly in the scenes of Church's early life is the agonized interdependence of the empowered and the powerless. Nearly every episode and relationship conveys both "the fury of the oppressed and the used" and the relativity of oppressed and oppressor, that is, the ease with which individuals and groups tend to move back and forth between the two conditions. In political discussions, king and Parliament are alternately perceived as controlling and controlled. Church's father, himself a former victim of the social hierarchy, clings now to his property, rejecting and abusing the class from which he emerged: "Why, they'll turn everyone against all the nobility and clergy and gentry in the land and destroy the monarchy itself. That is not what we meant when we started—to trim the tree, not strike so near the root" (63). Johnny Church, near the top of the ladder at his Henlow home, slips, at fourteen, to the bottom at Oxford, where he is scorned by "the lordy boys from Lords and Magdalen" (59) and whipped and jailed for his "newfangled democratical notions" (60). Even the servants at Lacy House momentarily assume a tyrannical role as they linger over the slaughter of a trussed hog in one of the novel's most overtly emblematic scenes: "The first huge hog was trussed up by its hind feet, screaming; its heavy head trying still to tusk the men who came near, its prick long and hard with fury. One of the men leaned forward and hit the member until it seemed to fence with him. They stood in a circle around the animal and moved away to make room as the squire and the two bloodied and dung-covered boys walked among them, still panting from the fight" (35). "This violent physical reaction of the pig against being trussed and tied," notes Joyce Coyne Dyer, "metaphorically represents the very emotions Sir Valentine's servants feel for their master."[7] More ominous, given the direction events are soon to take, is the readiness of those servants to assume Sir Valentine's position and to transform their "deadened patient fury" at victimization into a lust to victimize.

Johnny Church's life is punctuated by two great moments of defiance and self-definition, the first of which occurs on his sixteenth birthday and signals the end of his childhood. His father, he discovers, plans to flood the local village to create "a fine new vista in the Italian manner" (65) and in so doing to displace the peasants whose ties to the land are virtually organic. For once, the cloak of relativism is stripped from truth and value, and, Church later recalls, "What I had to do did keep showing itself to me, and I did not like it" (65). What he does, by cropping his hair, clipping his gentleman's lace, and refusing to kneel and doff his hat, is publicly defy the authority of his father. After a brief confrontation, he leaves home to join the Parliamentary army, stopping on the way at Lacy House, where he gathers provisions, bids farewell to his dying uncle, and is seduced by his still-young aunt. Unbeknownst for some time to both Church and the reader, this coupling produces a son, Jonathan Lacy, the great-grandfather of the Jonathan Lacey in *O Beulah Land,* who "would have been typical of those young men who went to Virginia in the 1670's" (256), and thus in effect initiates the subsequent four novels. So this first rebellion becomes, like the second, an act not just of separation but of creation, though what will be primarily ideological in the latter case is here primarily familial.

The remainder of the novel describes Johnny Church's four years with the Parliamentary army, though in no continuous or historically comprehensive way. Because Church's memory creates the structure and directs the focus of the narrative, it seems fitting that the novel jump abruptly from one major incident to the next and almost ignore events of great national but little personal significance, such as the exe-

7. Dyer, "Taproots History," 32.

cution of the king. Church recalls the gathering of thousands of Parliamentary soldiers at Marston; his initial experience of battle at Naseby (called by Garrett "as fine a piece of writing of the first confused experience of combat . . . as any we have"); the debates among rebel factions at Putney; and the election of himself and Thankful Perkins as Agitators, or popular representatives, at Salisbury.[8] Finally, as remembrance catches up with present circumstances, he describes in the novel's longest sustained episode his capture and confrontation with Cromwell at Burford. During this almost dizzying progression of intense experiences, the certainty that impelled Church's separation from his father is first lost amid "a tangled web of men and colors" (92) and ultimately, in the climactic encounter, regained with greater clarity and at a greater cost.

The Burford section of the novel is both its most emotionally charged and its most ideologically explicit. Cromwell, weary of negotiating with dissenting factions of his army, lures them to a meeting at Burford, where they are easily captured and imprisoned. As influential Agitators, Church and Perkins are used as object lessons and offered the choice of either recantation, by urging their fellow soldiers uncritically to follow Cromwell, or execution. For Church the choice is not only a moral one, between convenience and conscience, but once again the more agonizing one between family and freedom, paternal love and rejection, with Cromwell reenacting the role of Johnny's demanding father: "Why, I can feel my own heart heavy that he bragged of me and so long with my soul to turn again for blessing, to placate this man and all fathers, to be remembered by him as he sits by the fire at evening with his bandy leg upon a stool, and watch him smile a blessing at the thought of me. All I need do is turn again and doff my hat, and this man waits so patiently for me to turn" (211). The complex and politically consequential choice is reduced for Church to the choice, once again, of whether or not to "doff his hat" to a figure of seductive but unjust authority. He reaffirms now his earlier selection of conscience and freedom.

The closing moments of the novel deserve special note, both because they are among the most achingly powerful in the entire quintet and

8. Garrett, *Understanding Mary Lee Settle*, 49.

because they embody the importance of Johnny Church's decision in a series of vivid physical images. As Church goes to his death, the clarity of ethical and political vision that forced his rejection of Cromwell transforms itself into a literal clarity of perception: "I must walk carefully across the grass, for it is slippery with blood and dew. I turn. I face the spire now. Why is that cow lowing? It is too early to milk. She must be in calf" (254). And moral courage becomes physical courage: "This doublet is too heavy for the shot. I must take it off and spread my arms so that the shot will find true" (254). This language-oriented novel ends with an exhaustion of language and with an image of a deified Johnny Church stepping, Christ-like, toward his executioners.

> What can I say who have said so much? Shoot true, and God forgive us for what we do to one another? Thankful has said it all. You are unwise.
> There are no words. I am empty.
> I stretch wide my arms.
> I step forward. (254)

This is the moment and the image that haunts the reader and defines the characters of the subsequent twelve hundred pages.

To the reader of nineteenth-century historical fiction, there must inevitably be something familiar about this plot and these conflicts. Perhaps because *Prisons* is Settle's only novel set entirely in Europe, it is the one with the clearest ties to the tradition of European historical fiction defined most influentially by Lukács and exemplified by the works of Scott, Dickens, Stendahl, Tolstoy, and the like. For these novelists, the dialectical nature of the historical process is best dramatized at moments when forces of conflict are most violent and most starkly opposed, that is, at moments of war or revolution, so these typically become the setting of major historical fiction. Civil wars or wars in which participants are likely to feel divided loyalties have seemed particularly well suited to demonstrating the opposition of impulses not just among but within individuals. Moreover, the spectacle of a nation or culture rending itself apart attaches a terrifying moral to novels so often intended to be instructive to the contemporary reader. Settle begins the Foreword to *Prisons,* for example, by asserting that during the seventeenth century, "ideas, politics, and religion were in greater ferment than in any century before our own" (5).

Johnny Church is in many respects the quintessential hero of historical fiction, an amalgam of characteristics seen elsewhere in the protagonists of Scott, Dickens, Thackeray, and their less illustrious followers. Like most of Scott's protagonists, he is one of those "decent and average" men whose "purely individual traits of character . . . are brought into a very complex, very live relationship with the age in which they live." Poised between commoners and kings and between competing social and political forces, the heroes of traditional historical novels are meant to embody in their personal struggles the conflicts and contradictions of their time. Typically they come into direct or indirect contact with what Avrom Fleishman calls "world-historical figures," or actual figures of great historical importance, and find their lives "shaped by [these] figures and other influences in a way that epitomizes the process of change going forward in the society as a whole."[9] Johnny Church is surely at the center of events: not quite a nobleman yet clearly no peasant, landowner by birth yet democrat by inclination, hero-worshipper yet individualist, he seems perfectly suited to act as a kind of battleground on which the major conflicts of his time can be played out. Even as a child, he defines his world as "the world between the houses" (53). His infatuation with and then victimization by Cromwell, moreover, are meant to symbolize the relations between the country, or at least one segment of it, and that charismatic leader. No other character in the quintet is more thoroughly representative of his own historical moment.

The problems with these Waverley-like heroes have been documented often enough. Too easily the average shades into the mediocre, the representative becomes the simplistic, and the centrally placed protagonist is overwhelmed within his own story by the more individualized, more captivating characters at either extreme. As characters such as Edward Waverley, Charles Darnay, and Henry Esmond become more representative of their times, suggests Harry Shaw, "they also tend to become thinner as representations of 'inwardly complex' human beings."[10] One traditional aim of the historical novelist, to epitomize an age within a particular consciousness, seems to work against the traditional aim of the realistic novelist to individualize the protagonists sufficiently for them to rise above their companions and milieus. Settle

9. Lukács, *Historical Novel,* 36, 47; Fleishman, *English Historical Novel,* 11.
10. Shaw, *Forms of Historical Fiction,* 49.

manages to combine Johnny Church's historical typicality with a complex, fully realized personality largely through her major stylistic deviation from the nineteenth-century model: the use of the first-person narrative. The difference between Johnny Church and Scott's protagonists is the difference between David Copperfield or Pip and the rest of Dickens' heroes; linguistic skill, perspicaciousness, and moral sensitivity, all revealed through the narrative voice, compensate for the absence of idiosyncratic or flamboyant behavior. What makes Church unique is not his final, fatal refusal to compromise (recall Darnay's selfless return to France) but the fact that his refusal is explained from the inside.

The other portrait in *Prisons* that strongly recalls the nineteenth century is that of Cromwell, a hard man in whom Settle detects "a kind of interior softness" (Appendix B, p. 158). As much as any figure from the past, Cromwell calls to mind the susceptibility of the previous century's historians and historical novelists to hero worship, that is, to see a few great men as set apart from their fellows to be the primary shapers of the historical process. For Carlyle, notes Basil Willey, "History is essentially Biography, and above all the Biography of Great Men"; of these great men, "Cromwell was the chief . . . because he was the soldier of God." Most nineteenth-century historical novels, especially in England, where Carlyle's influence was most profound, include at least one rather infatuated portrait of some great man or another. "No preacher," writes George Eliot, "ever had a more massive influence than Savonarola," and in *Romola* she makes the Italian friar the subject of a Carlylean study that typifies the genre: "His need of personal predominance, his labyrinthine allegorical interpretations of the Scriptures, his enigmatic visions, and his false certitude about the Divine intentions, never ceased, in his own large soul, to be ennobled by that fervid piety, that passionate sense of the infinite, that active sympathy, that clear-sighted demand for the subjection of selfish interests to the general good, which he had in common with the greatest of mankind." Like many of the heroes of history, Savonarola appears morally ambiguous, but his "large soul," his "passionate sense of the infinite," and his "clear-sighted" nature mark him as among "the greatest of mankind." The great man is not necessarily better than the ordinary in any ethical, intellectual, or physical sense; he is, however, demonstrably other than ordinary in being more prescient and more attuned to the complex movements of time and circumstance. Generally this otherness is discernible, if not definable, by all those who encounter him, as Savonarola's power is felt instinctively by "the mass of his audience."[11]

Settle's Cromwell is both faithfully re-created (his speeches are modeled carefully on his actual utterances) and granted a Carlylean, almost preternatural stature. The visual angle from which Johnny Church first sees his general, perched on a horse "high above," makes physical an emotional and spiritual awe:

> I saw him then, mighty Cromwell, setting his horse high above me, followed by only a few officers. He had dirty linen, and his hands and face were streaked with mud from hard riding. He was smiling down on Gideon. It was a sweet smile that belied the stern lines of his face. His eyes looked as a man's who falls into secret melancholies, apologetic, sodden eyes, with much need in them. I would have said a drunkard from them and from his swollen face, but it is not so—not for so common a lover as strong drink. (78)

Everything about Settle's picture of Cromwell emphasizes his mystery and magnitude: his description through the eyes of a worshipful young protagonist; his infrequent, hastily glimpsed appearances; his voice that is "quiet but still rings" (190). Certainly, like Savonarola, Cromwell seems at best morally ambiguous; "at once wily and sincere, an opportunist and a man of conviction," he plays the villain's role in the destruction of Johnny Church.[12] But the portrayal nonetheless embodies the notion that certain men and women are unusually sensitive to the movements of history and to the implications of their own roles in the historical process and at the same time appear mysteriously compelling to those around them. Cromwell's melancholic, sodden eyes, his most striking feature, are pained by visions of his own appearance to his contemporaries and to the future. Acutely self-conscious, he "speaks to his own image in the glass" (203) and listens "for an inner answer he cannot hear" (79).

Ultimately, however, Settle's characterization of Cromwell undermines more than it endorses the great-man theory of history, as the reader, along with Johnny Church, is gradually educated out of hero

11. Basil Willey, *Nineteenth Century Studies: Coleridge to Matthew Arnold* (New York, 1949), 126, 130; George Eliot, *Romola* (1863; rpr. New York, 1980), 358–59.

12. Vance, "Historical Voices," 404.

worship. Cromwell rightly recognizes his importance but not his significance; he senses his own presence at the center of cataclysmic events but has no real power to direct or predict the movement of those events or the way they will be understood by future generations. Much less space in *Prisons* is given to Cromwell, who appears in the end an isolated and compelling peculiarity, than to the dissatisfactions, debates, and petty jealousies that, for Settle, were the real causes of the Puritan revolution. Church, as a participant in the historical moment, is only vaguely aware of its implications, but to the idea that average men and personal motives shape the future he seems particularly sensitive. He observes: "Of all the wars men fight, civil wars rise from no great single matters, actions of the king or Parliament, or this or that, not down here in the sullen mud. They start in houses, houses like my father's, and in men's breasts where outrage grows and grows, and blooms in the heart, and bursts over a countryside" (16). Watching the quiet lamentations of two peasants, he is ominously prophetic when he says of them, "Ones like Lazarus and Charity will sit long in rooms like this and cry tears down, dumb tears louder than any howling and crocodile weeping for policy, and they will change the world" (154). Here, more than in Cromwell's tragically futile attempts to mold events, can be discerned the mainsprings of history.

Between them, Cromwell and Johnny Church act out the central drama in *Prisons* and lay the thematic groundwork for the entire quintet. They embody and articulate the initial version of the "debate between authority and conscience" that takes place in each of the novels and, in so doing, make explicit the issues at stake in the conflict and the ideological basis of each position.[13] One's sympathy in this confrontation lies almost entirely with Church for reasons artistic (he is the narrator), emotional (he is the underdog), and political (he is the freedom fighter). Although Settle intentionally steers her readers toward this perspective, she means them as well to see or feel the defensibility of each viewpoint and to understand why most democratic action takes place within the middle ground circumscribed by the two ideological extremes. Paradoxically, moreover, Cromwell and Church are shown as more drawn to one another, more alike, than either is to those prepared to compromise: "We weigh each other, he and I," Church

13. Garrett, *Understanding Mary Lee Settle,* 50.

observes, "and both are annoyed by the watching of the others" (212).

Cromwell is representative not just of authoritarian might but of the various and subtler guises power may take in its attempts to conquer and co-opt those who oppose it. He resorts to execution only after trying virtually every appeal to reason and emotion through which the powerful have traditionally attempted to overcome the rebellious. He asks for more time: "I want no more than unity in this army and peace and safety. After that we can treat" (212). He tries to lure them into complicity: "If there is such iniquity as this you write of among us, help us to find it out that we may remove such sad rebukes as you have placed upon us" (210). He appeals to their concern for their companions: "You have much influence among these plain misguided men. You can stop a slaughter of them" (211). He calls for their sympathy: "I have not slept this night for thinking of thee" (210). He insists on the necessity of order: "Where will it stop, this democratical notion? If all have rights who have no property and interest but the interest in breathing, you will bring anarchy" (204). The failure of these appeals is testimony not to Cromwell's insufficiency or insincerity as an advocate, for "he blots from my mind," Church admits, "any belief that he has not acted from the bottom of his innocence" (210), but to the determination of Church and Perkins to allow no argument to alter their absolute faith in the justice of their ideals.

Those ideals, and by extension the ideals of Church's successors throughout the quintet, are relatively few and straightforward, beginning with the assertion that "what is done to anyone may be done to everyone" (61). These words, actually spoken by John Lilburne before the Star Chamber in 1638 and quoted directly in the novel, suggest why the individual actions of Church and Perkins are so resonant with meaning: both men acknowledge the connection, by analogy or direct influence, between themselves and the larger community to which they belong. Here and throughout Settle's fiction, there is no escaping the responsibility for one's decisions by insisting on their personal or inconsequential nature. Because one cannot predict how seemingly personal choices and actions will affect the fate of others, one must always behave as if those choices and actions are communally significant. Church takes almost literally Lilburne's description of Englishmen as "all members of one body" (61), characterizing the mass of Parliamentary soldiers as "a single body" (94) and likening the continuous circulation of the blood, recently discovered by William Harvey, to the "rushing and circular" (62) movement of men and of the universe itself. This belief in connectedness is the foundation on which the novel's two other central ideals are erected.

The first of these is captured in Church's claim that "we must accept as hallowed the unblessings of our fathers" (67): we must, that is, accept as beneficial and even necessary the separation from paternal authority and, by extension, from all authority that seeks to make our decisions for us. Such a separation need not be as absolute as Church's separation from his father or as mortal as his separation from Cromwell, but rarely will it be achieved without pain. The placement of the paternal relationship at the center of *Prisons* forges yet another connection to nineteenth-century imaginative history. "Essentially," writes Steven Marcus, "*Barnaby Rudge* contemplates only one kind of personal relation—that of father and son." With some qualification, the same might be said of *Waverley, Old Mortality, Henry Esmond,* and even *Past and Present,* where relations between sons and actual or surrogate fathers dramatize, sometimes metaphorically, sometimes literally, social, political, and psychological conflict. The Oedipal struggle between father and son neatly mirrors the ambivalence of the revolutionary confrontations usually at the heart of the historical novel, so that, in the classic example, Edward Waverley's rebellion against England becomes as well a rebellion against his guardian and the pressure of family tradition. As one would expect in largely conservative texts, however, the rebellion against paternal authority is rarely absolute: rather than separating himself entirely from fathers or rulers, the protagonist sifts through a group of more or less adequate mentors before arriving at a state of acceptable obedience. The conciliatory endings of Dickens and Scott call for the establishment of social and familial order headed by figures of beneficent power. Although the need for the father is equally powerful in *Prisons*—"father's a fathom's deeper need than lover" (242)—no reconciliation can occur because the need for freedom takes precedence, even if that freedom carries with it feelings of loss and existential terror. "Johnny," notes Dyer, "knows he must remain fatherless to remain free."[14]

14. Steven Marcus, *Dickens: From Pickwick to Dombey* (New York, 1965), 184; Dyer, "Taproots History," 36.

This ideal virtually implies, as a corollary, a second one: "Freedom's no fine thing," Church insists, even as he is about to die for it. "It is as simple as the opening of a door, or a ceasing of persuasions upon you, or a blessing" (222). *Prisons* insists on freedom not as one among a group of desirable conditions but as the particular condition without which most other desirable ones are impossible, as what Vance calls "a practical condition of decent human life."[15] Its rarity is attributable not to its undesirability but to its cost, for of course Settle insists here as elsewhere on the often staggering "price of freedom." Because so many characters in the Beulah quintet will be forced to decide whether to pay that price, it seems especially important at the start, in the definitive situation of Church and Perkins, to make the choice clear and the price high.

Both the choice and the price are clarified further through repeated references to the story of Antigone and Creon. Although this myth, as I have already suggested, lends meaning to the entire quintet, its relevance is most profound in *Prisons,* where Oxford-educated Johnny Church explicitly likens his situation to Antigone's and models his decision on hers.[16] Thus the myth functions not merely as an allusion directed at the reader but as an element of Church's consciousness that directly affects his actions; it is not merely an analogue to the plot but a part of the plot. Antigone's story teaches, first of all, the importance of recognizing when the moment to act has arrived, as Francis White, Church's officer and idol, argues at Putney: "Even Antigone, he said, sat quiet and played the pretty lass in the palace of Creon until the time had come, a fifteen-year-old girl of no import when she stood there holding a little dirt in her small hand, but when she turned her narrow wrist, she shook the state" (118). Later, confronted by Cromwell's "What else can I do?" (192), Church recalls Antigone's momentous sprinkling of dust on the unburied corpse of her brother Polyneices:

15. Vance, "Historical Voices," 412.

16. Schafer considers Church's use of Antigone anachronistic, since in the mid-seventeenth century the Greek version of Sophocles had not yet been published in England (Schafer, "History Darkly," 86). A Latin translation by the poet Thomas Watson (1557–1592) had been published in 1581, however, and might plausibly have been read by a student at Oxford. Also worth noting is that Francis White, a far more advanced scholar than Church, introduces the myth into the story and into the forefront of Church's consciousness.

> That is the question that Creon asked her, the girl with the dirt clutched in her fist; her uncle asked Antigone that final question, and she had no answer for him, for his words took place somewhere else, stars away from her, and so she turned her wrist and it turns still. Francis, you gave me greater gift than you knew with the myths you told me. She did not need to wait so politic as you think. The time came and met her. That's all that stands against their power to damn and diminish us, the turning of a wrist. (193)

Antigone reminds Church of his freedom to disobey, of his inability to predict how meaningful even a small act of disobedience may prove to be, and, most generally, of the potential for a gesture to retain a virtually timeless significance. It seems fitting that a person as sensitive as Church to the importance of language and symbols should, in the end, pattern his actions after those of a character in a play.

On another level, *Prisons* is a meditation on the relations between the individual and history, or between free will and historical determinism. Like William Butler Yeats in "Leda and the Swan" ("Did she put on his knowledge with his power / Before the indifferent beak could let her drop?"), Settle wonders in *Prisons* how thoroughly individuals can understand and control the large historical movements in which they are participants. Informing classic historical fiction is the belief that individuals in the past, and by implication those in the present, can consciously, for better or worse, affect the course of events, since without such faith the writing of instructive history would be fruitless. George Eliot's call for imaginative history that "might help the judgement greatly with regard to present and future events" surely implies that history, if properly read, is at least partially controllable. Historical narrative unsustained by such a belief is likely to degenerate into the parodic despair of *Israel Potter*, which teaches only that "men who act and men who are acted upon are equally liable to frustration and defeat" and ends with its protagonist "repulsed in efforts" and "faded out of memory."[17]

Settle's view of the relations between human beings and history should probably be located somewhere between the optimism of Eliot and the hopelessness of Melville. To Church's admission that "a man can go with the tide, not rule it" (127), she has added the qualification

17. Edward Rosenberry, *Melville* (Boston, 1979), 108; Herman Melville, *Israel Potter: His Fifty Years of Exile* (1854; rpr. Evanston, 1982), 169.

that "he has to be intelligent enough to know when the tide's coming in" (Appendix B, p. 165), sensitive enough to gauge its strength and direction. One of the ways of controlling history is to recognize that one's own power to do so is limited: whereas those who trust in their ability to bend events wholly to their own will, like Cromwell, will inevitably fail, those who acknowledge the presence of forces beyond their control or comprehension, like Church, may in the end effect some meaningful change. *Prisons* points to the paradoxical truth that the historical process both is larger than the efforts of individual men and, potentially, can be shifted dramatically by the smallest, most unportentous actions, events, and decisions. Only rarely, however, will such dramatic shifts be noticeable to those who cause them. According to Settle, the "pulsing line of history" in the quintet is "the history of people who caused some essential social change despite their belief that they'd failed," and among its central themes is the realization that "we know more about the past than the people who were living in it knew when it was the present" (Appendix B, pp. 159, 162). Church is distinguished by being that rare actor in history wise enough to confess his ignorance: "Already," he remembers, "there was a new pattern if we could have seen it, but we were so blinded by success that most of us saw it not" (114).

Insistently Church likens the rush of history to two sorts of natural, continuous movement: the flow of water and the slow growth of vegetation. Both images, especially the former, figure prominently in the quintet as a whole. Here, they become the most effective means of conveying that mixed sense of helplessness and control, ignorance and insight, that characterizes Church's (and Settle's) view of the historical process. From the opening paragraph, which situates the reader in the "great flat valley of the Thames," water, particularly in the form of rivers and streams, seems to course just beneath the surface of Church's narrative, carrying men in its currents as the Thames carries boats "like butterflies" (115). The flow is powerful, ceaseless, and, most important, as unpredictable as the movements of history: "A stream," like a memory or the result of an action, sometimes "disappears and flows underneath a meadow and then finds a fall to release it so that it seems to come from no place like a new spring, a holy well, and courses stronger in new lands" (51). "What seemed a flat morass held hidden current we could not yet fathom," Church later recalls. "Looking back now, I can see that there were streams, barely perceptible, as some that move the water here as we cross it" (98).

Images of vegetation resemble yet counterbalance these images of water, embodying control rather than powerlessness and inevitability rather than unpredictability. The growth of a plant, like the flowing of a river, is natural and continuous, yet the seed or origin of the former is more easily discoverable and the eventual product or endpoint more predictable. What is significant, the vegetative imagery is used almost exclusively to describe the rebels, who appear to fail yet who are themselves the seeds of important, inevitable change. "I saw us," Church says, "as plants growing upward with the strength surging from below as we reached our arms toward heaven" (84); "it was like early spring, when the frail shoots seem so isolated in the first flow of mud and dark, dark earth" (102); "new leaders were growing in all that rich soil of disaffection" (105). "Oh, Oliver," he eventually laments, "you grew us into this and now do hate your harvest" (138). In these interrelated images is embodied the core of Settle's philosophy of history: the flow of events, like the flow of water, will take place regardless of human attempts to control or predict it, but man in history, like the wise cultivator of the land, may use this flow to nurture carefully chosen and beneficial fruit.

The point at which the central subjects of *Prisons* intersect is the resonant image of enclosure for which the novel is named. Johnny Church alludes to the prison, literally or figuratively, better than two dozen times and, in doing so, manages at once to recall the nineteenth-century tradition on which the story is based and to provide a physical embodiment of the social, political, and historical forces that impose limits on personal freedom. The modern coercive prison, as opposed to the classical dungeon, Foucault has pointed out, was in effect invented in the nineteenth century, and not surprising, it was incorporated almost immediately into the discourse of the time as an image of peculiar force and visibility. Hayden White summarizes Foucault's argument: "[Nineteenth- and twentieth-century penal systems] represent a social authority that masks itself behind professions of humanistic concerns for the citizen, humanitarian principles of social organization, and altruistic ideals of service and enlightenment. But this authority, as sovereign in practice as any absolute monarch claimed to be in theory, seeks to make society into an extended prison, in which discipline becomes an end in itself; and conformity to a norm that governs every aspect of life, and especially desire, becomes the only principle of both law and morality." White does well to note that "this sounds very much like the kind of ranting we normally associate with conservative opponents of the power of the centralized state," but the fact remains that many nineteenth-century novelists, from Scott in *The Heart of Mid-Lothian* to Dickens in *Little Dorrit* to Tolstoy in *Resurrection,* used the prison precisely in this way as an embodiment of economic entrapment, psychological repression, and oppressive social control.[18] For historical novelists, concerned with the pull between historical inevitability and the potential for even one person to shift the current of events, prisons and prison breaks were especially suggestive. The action in both *Barnaby Rudge* and *A Tale of Two Cities,* for instance, builds to an explosive prison revolt, during which desperate individuals battle against a maelstrom that seems irresistible and without controlling principle. Although in the end the violence subsides, order is restored, and the worthy and unworthy take their appropriate places on either side of the restraining wall, the image of the prison as an instrument of arbitrary power and as a thwarter of desire never dissipates.

Almost from the beginning, Church imagines as prisonlike all forms of physical, emotional, and ideological restriction and enclosure: his schoolroom is "that prison" (29); his father and uncle sequester themselves within "the prisons of their houses" (30); his widowed aunt is cared for at Henlow, "charity's prison" (106); the king dwells "in a prison that no one called a prison" (112); the house in Burford commandeered by Cromwell becomes a "prison of Delft china and pretty carvings" (202). This almost obsessive use of the term gradually broadens its meaning, transforming it into the metaphor that comes to dominate Church's speculations during his climactic confrontation with authority. "We are," he complains, "in prisons of other men's beliefs" (222). His political goal, and the intention behind his refusal to compromise, are defined by Thankful Perkins as, awaiting execution, he

18. See Michel Foucault, *Discipline and Punish: The Birth of the Prison,* trans. Alan Sheridan (New York, 1977), 231–33; White, *Content of the Form,* 128.

reads aloud from the book of Isaiah: "To open the blind eyes, and bring out the prisoners from the prison, and them that sit in the darkness of the prison house" (245). The prisons to which the title of the novel finally refers are not physical ones but, like William Blake's "mind-forg'd manacles," the psychological and emotional ones through which authority attempts to shape the beliefs and principles of those under its control. Among Cromwell's errors is his confusion of these two forms of coercion. External imprisonment may in certain circumstances be necessary to prevent a slide into anarchy, but internal imprisonment is never, for that reason or any other, justifiable.

"Essentially," Settle has said, "*Prisons* reverberates through the whole of the five volumes," for "there are different prisons of the South, prisons of the family, prisons of decision, and so on, that run all the way through" (Appendix B, p. 166). This first novel serves in part as the quintet's dictionary or glossary of terms, establishing at the start the exact meaning, within this particular series of novels, of general concepts such as freedom, authority, and responsibility. In fact the earliest seeds of *Prisons* were linguistic ones: Settle discovered that Thomas Jefferson had the name *Lilburne* inscribed on a ring and that the start of the motto of the American Civil Liberties Union ("For what is done to any one may be done to every one") was taken from Lilburne's Star Chamber address, and she began to suspect that "our language, our language of democracy" (Appendix B, p. 161), may have had its beginning an ocean away in the relatively obscure Leveller movement. This suspicion, more than anything else, led to the eventual expansion of the trilogy into the quintet.

Nonetheless, *Prisons* stands on its own best of all the novels in the final sequence not only because its setting and characters are least intertwined with the rest but because the trajectory of its plot is clearest and its themes most emphatically presented. This product of Settle's recognition that *O Beulah Land* and *Know Nothing* would benefit from a clarifying prologue itself requires no prologue or epilogue. In part for this reason, *Prisons* may be Settle's most fully realized work of fiction, the one in which story, character, and language work together most seamlessly to make the reader first "leave the present," then "come back into the present with a psychic and emotional knowledge" of the represented past (Appendix B, p. 157). Certainly it is her most concentrated, most relentlessly moving work, and Johnny Church is her most archetypal character. Despite his firm grounding in the language and habits of his time, he becomes for the contemporary reader what Antigone is for him: a timeless, alluring embodiment of the nature of freedom. In the only non-American novel in the quintet, ironically, one finds the character who most precisely defines its American quality.

# *O Beulah Land* and *Know Nothing* Burying the Past 4

One of the more remarkable characteristics of the Beulah quintet is the fullness with which the structure and concerns of the whole are anticipated by the earliest volumes, despite the extended period of composition and the fact that, at the start, Mary Lee Settle had not envisioned a five-novel series. *O Beulah Land* and *Know Nothing* required virtually no revision to fit securely into a long, tightly knit sequence completed more than two decades after their composition. Not only is their overall quality consistent with that of the subsequently published novels, but so, too, are their dominant characters, images, themes, and approach to the central subjects of freedom and history. In some ways these early productions of a young novelist are more impressive than their successors, since they were composed at a time when historical fiction had fallen into virtually total disrepute and when the narrative and stylistic experiments they represent would have seemed less familiar to the reader than they are today. No Fowles or Doctorow had prepared the public of 1956 for *O Beulah Land*.

The two novels share more than their period of composition. Despite the gap of 63 years between the end of one and the beginning of the next, the events of the two seem more contiguous than those of any other works in the quintet. On the whole, the chronological separation between the novels in the quintet gradually shrinks: there is a gap of 105 years between the end of *Prisons* in 1649 and the earliest episodes of *O Beulah Land* in 1754; of 63 years between 1774, the end of *O Beulah Land,* and 1837, the start of *Know Nothing;* of 51 years between the end of *Know Nothing* in 1861 and the action of *The Scapegoat,* which begins in 1912; and of 48 years between *The Scapegoat* and the episodes set earliest, in 1960, in *The Killing Ground.* Still, because of the increasing pace of cultural change, the historical discontinuities between the later volumes appear more radical. The case is different for the early volumes. The physical setting of *O Beulah Land* is still powerfully present, if transformed, in *Know Nothing;* the characters and events of the former are continually being recalled in the latter, both explicitly by the characters themselves and allusively in the narrative; the familial and geographic distinctions established in the first still largely hold in the second. By the time *The Scapegoat* begins, a decade into the twentieth century, the landscape has been reshaped almost beyond recognition, and the social and familial hierarchies that ordered this world in the eighteenth and nineteenth centuries have melted away or dramatically changed configuration. If there is a moment in the quintet when the rush of events appears to have slowed, it is in the early sections of *Know Nothing,* when the world created at the end of *O Beulah Land,* what Roger Shattuck calls "a marriage of the real and the ideal in a reasonably harmonious community," seems for a time to have been nurtured and preserved.[1]

Whereas *Prisons, The Scapegoat,* and *The Killing Ground,* moreover, are noticeably different from one another in structure and style, *O Beulah Land* and *Know Nothing* form a relatively consistent structural and stylistic whole. Both works weave huge casts of significant characters into a third-person narrative whose focal point shifts regularly. Both make a central male character, Jonathan Lacey and then Johnny Catlett, the focal point more often than any other figure. Unlike *Prisons* and *The Scapegoat* especially, both re-create the spoken language of the represented time exclusively within the dialogue of the characters; their narrative voice is Settle's own, complex, imagistic, and meticulous. Both are divided into three books that span panoramically more than two decades, though each book covers in detail only a rather narrow period, ranging from two days to five years. If these characteristics seem con-

1. Shattuck, Introduction, xi.

ventional in comparison to the more radical narrative experiments Settle was subsequently to attempt, one only need recall that, even so, many early readers of these novels shared William Peden's perception that their whirl of character and incident was "confusing."[2]

The genesis of *O Beulah Land* is worth reviewing, both because it represents the genesis of the entire quintet and because it offers a detailed model of how Settle customarily discovers and develops her material. Like most of her novels, this one began not with an idea but with a visual image, precise yet at the start largely unexplained. Settle recalls her original vision in this way: "The image was of a woman lost in the Endless Mountains. I saw her stripped down to nothing but life and survival. She had no memory, she had a direction, and that was all."[3] Eventually this image was to blossom into the ordeal of Hannah Bridewell depicted in the prologue to *O Beulah Land*. Initially, however, it was merely a vision of need and deprivation: "I wanted the reader and myself to experience the pure luxury of having any kind of food and any kind of shelter." Once the image had been fixed in the eighteenth century, Settle recognized that she needed, as she puts it, "to construct a historic memory" of that period before she could write convincingly, from the inside, of its people and conflicts. This she accomplished here, as in all the other novels of the quintet, by immersing herself in primary source materials, spending ten months reading documents, memoirs, and correspondence written prior to 1774. More than an academic exercise (she took not a single note), this intensive studying was an attempt to make personal and instinctive the habits of thought and language that characterized the American settlers of the eighteenth century. Only after this "ambience of memory" (Appendix B, p. 157) had been created did the book's outline itself begin to take shape.

The novel that arose from this image and the subsequent research is set primarily in pre–Revolutionary War Virginia, though one early chapter takes place in the alleys and prisons of London. Its broad subjects are the settling of western Virginia, which in this telling bears little resemblance to the commonly accepted American myth, and the evo-

2. William Peden, Review of *Know Nothing*, in *Saturday Review*, November 5, 1960, p. 33.

3. This and subsequent quotations in the paragraph are taken from remarks prepared by Mary Lee Settle, taped in Charlottesville, Va., in 1986. The tape is in my possession.

lution of the conflicts that would lead to the revolt of the colonies against their English rulers. As in *Prisons,* these very large issues are explored mainly through the carefully rendered lives of very ordinary people, though here the cast of important characters is more sizable and the effect more panoramic and comprehensive. Rather than hearing the first-person voice of Johnny Church, one encounters in *O Beulah Land* a third-person voice that penetrates the minds of men and women of a variety of personalities and from a fairly wide range of social and economic backgrounds. The longer period of time covered in *O Beulah Land,* from 1754 to 1774, allows as well for a clearer demonstration of generational distinctions: the four characters who dominate the first half of the novel all have children who differ noticeably from their parents and who themselves become important characters. As in *Prisons,* the fictional lives intertwine with actual historical events and people (including, briefly, George Washington), though none here plays nearly so prominent a role as Cromwell and his campaigns play in Church's narrative. In breadth, at least, *O Beulah Land* resembles more closely than does *Prisons* the sweeping historical fiction of the nineteenth century and the conventional historical sagas of the American frontier.

That the novel is far from conventional, however, is demonstrated almost immediately in the "impressionistic, imagistically-compacted" prologue with which it begins. George Garrett calls this description of Hannah Bridewell wandering lost in the mountains of western Virginia, then stumbling upon the solitary homestead of Jeremiah Catlett, "virtuoso" writing; certainly it is the section of the quintet that most insistently calls attention to its own style by re-creating in the imagery and the structure of the prose the consciousness of a "haunted, chased creature, mindless with panic" (6).[4] At the start the reader is made to share the slowly diminishing confusion of the central character, as visual fragments, "a single footprint" and "a thin, rootlike white arm" (3), gradually cohere into "a small something alive," then "a woman" (4), then, almost ten pages in, "Hannah." Soon one is engulfed by the winding Faulknerian prose as Hannah is engulfed by the lush vegetation of the mountains:

4. Vance, "History Inherited, History Created," 44; Garrett, *Understanding Mary Lee Settle,* 52.

> When the papaw fell the woman crept out of the tree, watching where her stiffened limbs set her feet, and grabbed it from the ground so fiercely with her cold hand that the smoky blue skin broke and yellow pulp squished between her fingers. Where she had come from there had been not even sweet papaws, only a choking mass of tangled and insidious laurel hugging her dress; rhododendron run wild over and under, making a strong mat which rose almost to tree height, mile upon mile of thick snaking roots, like the unkempt head of some insane giant. For two days she had stumbled, fought, thrust her body against the unyielding mass, without food, without water, in a maze of God, leaving a thin trail of linsey behind her in the selfish, high undergrowth, while above her head and out of sight the wild moving tops of the plants lifted their handsome black-green swirls of leaves and tried to charm the sun. (5)

Settle's prose, particularly in her early novels, tends to combine spare sensual precision, as in the description of the fragile, "smoky blue" fruit, with a metaphoric density that expands and further clarifies nearly every image. In effect, the language conveys at the same time a sense of the character's mind and a sense of an authorial mind capable of likening wild rhododendrons to the "unkempt head of some insane giant" or the wilderness to a "maze of God." However visceral one's experience of a character's anguish or excitement, it never fully obscures an awareness of Settle's controlling persona.

In two important ways the prologue prefigures not just the rest of *O Beulah Land* but the remaining novels in the quintet. Settle's historical fiction tends to be antiromantic, in the sense that it attempts to strip away the layers of imagination and desire that prevent, on both an individual and a cultural level, clear vision of the past and present. Many of her most surprising scenes are designed to deconstruct the mythologized version of the past that has been constructed and perpetuated by the historical romance, particularly, in *O Beulah Land* and *Know Nothing,* the powerful American myths of the frontier and the antebellum South. The story of "a homeland founded in the wilderness," according to George Dekker, has been for writers of American history and historical romance "the stuff out of which epics are made."[5] Because the situation in the prologue, in which pioneer woman and pioneer man find love in the wilderness, might lend itself so easily to romanticization, Settle presents it in graphic, antiromantic detail, to the

5. Dekker, *American Historical Romance,* 107–108.

extent that it resembles no historical fiction one is likely to have seen before. Starving, Hannah chokes and eats raw a squirrel whose "rodent teeth had bitten through the soft flesh of her thumb-pad until they met" (10); encountering the half-eaten carcass of a bear, she feeds like a desperate animal "until her head [swims], the strong fat running down her skinny body" (17). Her first spoken words, "Gawd, but I'm hongry" (9) and "I wisht I hadn't of et that whole critter" (11), are neither in style nor in subject the stuff of heroines. Jeremiah Catlett, sharing his cabin with a pig and her "squealing, glugging" litter (33), is equally unlike the conventional hero, and his coupling with Hannah at the close of the prologue works as Settle's ultimate repudiation of the historical romance. Jeremiah smells "the sweet smell of her sweat in the morning, and the fresh crushed tobacco dust which still clung to her face and hair" and takes her, "while . . . the piglets suckled" (55), in a deliberately parodic climax.

Beneath the squalor, however, Hannah and Jeremiah do embody a genuine heroism that also sets the tone for the fiction to come. The theme of the prologue, "survival against enormous odds," is among the central themes of a long work whose subjects include the struggle for survival both of the American ideal of freedom and of individuals who believe in that ideal.[6] Hannah Bridewell's battle against "the law which is so inevitable that it can crush the will and mind of a man" (5) is an extreme physical version of the battle joined by every protagonist in the quintet, and her need to "go on toward the mountains as we go toward death, inevitably moving, driven without choice" (11), is their need. Later, one discovers that Hannah's trek across the mountains began as an attempt to escape from the Indians who had captured her, so that her struggle to survive literally originated as a struggle for freedom. Jeremiah Catlett, similarly, has fled from bondage, his in the form of indentured servitude. Neither of these characters is capable of articulating the ideology of freedom as broadly as does Johnny Church, but perhaps for that reason they embody the fundamental urge for freedom more starkly.

The plot of *O Beulah Land,* or the collection of interwoven plots that make up its narrative, resists brief summation. The first book alone

6. Garrett, *Understanding Mary Lee Settle,* 52.

pays considerable attention to Hannah as she is transported from London to Alexandria, Virginia; to her fellow prisoners Squire Raglan, a handsome pickpocket, and Jarcey Pentacost, "scholar and printer" (81); to Peregrine Cockburn, a young British ensign, and his cousin Jonathan Lacey, a colonial captain; and to Lacey's wife Sally, aged sixteen and innocent as a child. None of these characters is granted clear primacy as events in 1755 build toward the defeat of General Edward Braddock by the French and Indians near Fort Duquesne, the most fully rendered historical incident in the novel. The battle seems an appropriate conclusion to the narrative of Book One, as the sense of events swirling beyond the control of individual characters culminates in a "current of panic" (129) that overwhelms and scatters the British army. Jonathan Lacey, trying to control himself and his troops, undergoes his own version of Hannah's helplessness in the woods: "He was caught up, buoyed, surrounded by a huge circle of a great gurgling animal shriek that swelled to a climax, stayed there, then ran along like fire down the hidden creek beds. It was as if the ear had split and there would never be any escape from that wild screaming. His horse plunged, reared, ridden by the noise and not by him" (127–28). The book ends with a harbinger of difficulties to come. Lacey, weary and distraught after the battle, reads his wife's letter about balls and watered silk and beats back his recognition of the difference between his "need of a wife" (140) and the "sixteen-year-old stranger, blond and elusive" (141), he had married.

Book Two, which picks up after the passage of eight years, focuses primarily on the struggle of Jonathan Lacey to found a plantation in the open valley west of the Endless Mountains. His main obstacles are his wife, who prefers the genteel, custom-bound life of the Tidewater, and the policies of the king, who has decreed a Proclamation Line along the mountain chain beyond which no subject is permitted to settle. The line was "established between Western Virginia and the Lands belonging to the Indian Nations of the Ohio Country," ostensibly "to quiet the Minds of the western Indians that the Intentions of His Majesty's Government are those of Honour with regard to the especial treaties made during the late War with our Indian Allies, in return for their Help in fighting off the French Tyranny" (174). In this novel's version of Johnny Church's defiance, Lacey (a direct descendant of Church) vows to "damn the Proclamation Line" (184) and settle nonetheless, an easy decision in comparison to those regarding his wife. For Sally Lacey, "habit is stronger than passion" (227), and the need for objects and manners to validate her being is more powerful than the need for land and autonomy. Even in an environment marked by extremes of deprivation, she experiences the loss of an English china plate as traumatic; even in the virtual absence of neighbors, the ability to make the right impression is important to her: "I always reckoned to live in brick or stone so folks'll know we're quality" (257). Jonathan Lacey's exhilaration at the founding of his home, named Beulah after a passage in Isaiah, is tempered by his growing realization that his wife will never adapt to it.

As the Laceys embody the relatively privileged, relatively rare westward migration of the gentry, Hannah and Jeremiah embody the more desperate movement of the masses. When encountered again in Book Two, they are still living in their isolated cabin, worn down by the work and the harshness of Jeremiah's fundamentalist religion. Their tired peace is shattered by the accidental arrival of Squire Raglan, become affluent trader, who revives in Hannah recollections of her earlier self and in Jeremiah, the escaped servant, fears of recapture. Out of "dire necessity" (204), in a fever of jealousy, terror, and deluded righteousness, Jeremiah shoots Raglan and buries the body in the woods. He moves his family to the west because "the border's a-gittin too near" (204), not groping, like Jonathan Lacey, for a dream but running from a fear. They land, nevertheless, in the same valley.

Hannah and Jeremiah serve not only as the forebears of a host of subsequent characters but as physical touchstones, or reference points, throughout the remainder of the quintet. The site of their cabin and the objects they carry with them to Beulah reappear in each of the later novels, tying together the narrative and revealing the way each age chooses to mythologize the past. Especially important are Raglan's grave, marked by a heap of stones, and the worn hearth of the cabin; a silver-handled riding crop, a combination tomahawk, scalping knife, and pipe, and a Bible, articles stolen by Raglan and taken from him in turn by Jeremiah; and a ruby, "red as a jewel for a king's crown" (19), fished by Hannah out of a creek bed during her journey across the mountains. What eventually happens to these objects (the tomahawk, for instance, is romanticized into a European heirloom) is for Settle a small version of what happens to the whole story of American expansion: the need for later generations to reinvent their history is directly proportional to its actual sordidness.

During Book Three, which runs from 1769 to 1774, the Beulah plantation becomes fixed in the landscape. Two counterbalanced political currents run through the book, as the settlers struggle on the one hand against the impositions of the English and on the other against the Shawnee and Cherokee Indians whose land is being appropriated. One of the more interesting themes of *O Beulah Land,* and one that seems to anticipate subsequent changes in the American consciousness, is the mistreatment of native Americans by the colonists, which demonstrates, like the events in *Prisons,* the fragility of the distinction between oppressed and oppressor. Unlike most representations of this period in historical fiction, *O Beulah Land* does not abandon what Robert Clark calls "the principles of objective historiography" in an attempt to disguise or transform the events of colonization.[7] Distinctions are drawn throughout the novel between self-preservation and racism, and Jarcey Pentacost, consistently a voice of conscience, is nearly burned alive for writing this injunction: "To move West on Broken Promises will mean more Bloodshed, more Revenge between the White man and the Red that can only be balanced by Death. Let us learn to govern Ourselves first. *Does it heal the Injustices of the Dispossessed that they Dispossess others as ruthlessly?*" (175). Again, Settle's impulse is to strip away from the past the comforting veneer of myth.

Already in Book Three the class distinctions that matter so much to Sally Lacey are beginning to disintegrate. The Laceys' daughter Sara marries, despite her mother's opposition, the Catletts' son Ezekiel. Because Jonathan and Sally leave—Jonathan to the House of Burgesses, Sally back to the Tidewater—and because their elder son Peregrine becomes a murderous Indian hunter and is disinherited, Beulah passes into Catlett hands scarcely a decade after its founding. The deaths of Hannah and Jeremiah during an Indian attack signal the shift in generations and the beginning of the process of covering over the past that will dominate *Know Nothing.* Ironically, the mixing of classes here will

7. Clark, *History, Ideology, and Myth,* 46.

produce more intense class consciousness, and Sally Lacey rather than Hannah Catlett will come to seem the progenitor of later behavior and values. Sally's mocking voice and "unbending will to conquer" (367) end the book.

Many of the controlling themes of *Prisons* are reiterated (or anticipated) in *O Beulah Land,* particularly in the story of Jonathan Lacey, who, like Johnny Church, plays the Antigone role in the novel's central crisis of conscience. Like Church, too, he is the character blessed with the most comprehensive understanding of the historical moment and with the ability to define the root causes of surface tensions: his Cromwell is the English government ("fools will try to force authority down our throats for the sake of authority" [248]), his dilemma, the conflict between old and new allegiances ("A man tugs many ways like a horse in the traces to ease his shoulders of his conflicting pulls of loyalty" [278]). He foresees the underlying personal origins of the American Revolution, as Church does of the English revolution: "Back a man to the wall with arrogance and contempt, and he strikes out blind in his roused pride" (248). A sign of the novel's early date of composition, though, may be the relative simplicity of the character of Lacey, who, from the moment he enters the story through his "calm" voice tinged with "amusement," "sense," and "authority," barely missteps. He may be the closest thing in the quintet to an unadulterated conventional hero, a kind of troubled Natty Bumppo, and seems for that reason comparatively wooden.

More interesting, and more typical of Settle, is Jeremiah Catlett, the other father of the quintet's subsequent generations and a character about whom one can make few easy moral judgments. Catlett is a frightening, possessed figure who murders in the name of God and treats harshly those few people he elects not to scorn altogether. Whereas in most fiction he would be marginalized as an eccentric, here he consistently plays a fairly prominent role and achieves, over time, a softening complexity and peculiarly heroic stature. For Catlett, more basically than for Lacey, independence is tied directly to survival: he embraces fundamentalism and even kills in an effort to find, "like a caught coon" (198), sufficient freedom from threat and from domination to live. If Jonathan Lacey defines the source of the American desire for freedom, Jeremiah Catlett embodies it, and if the conscience inherited from Lacey sets apart later generations of the family, the animal need inherited from Catlett ties them to the larger culture. One's response to Catlett modulates over the course of the novel along with the response of his wife, who initially is struck by his utter strangeness but can say unironically, near the end, "He's bent and he's broke, but he's still a nice, proud man" (298).

The most compelling figures in *O Beulah Land* are the women Hannah Bridewell and Sally Lacey, who begin a movement within the quintet toward increasing prominence for the female characters. *Prisons* includes only a handful of women in secondary roles; in *O Beulah Land* women are more numerous and more centrally placed; by the time of *The Killing Ground,* a woman will come to play the central part in the story—the Johnny part—and will be surrounded by a crowd of contrasting female types as Johnny Church is surrounded by male types. Partly this change is a consequence of the different sorts of experience being depicted in each novel: *Prisons* is essentially a story of war, *O Beulah Land,* of the frontier, and the later novels, of an increasingly domesticated and sexually integrated society. Partly, too, it represents a perceived shift in the frequency with which men and women play the Antigone role of self-sacrificial challenger of order and authority. If Settle, as she insists, is no feminist writer, for her concern is not exclusively or primarily female experience, she is nonetheless acutely interested in differentiating between the roles and responses of men and women within the American culture that has evolved over the past two centuries. She explores the different prescriptions and romanticized images against which each sex has had to struggle during the course of American history.

Hannah Bridewell and Sally Lacey embody two very different codes of behavior against which most of the later female characters can be measured. Hannah is a female animal, "stripped of accultured feminization" and unaffected by the self- and society-imposed restrictions that circumscribe the worlds of so many women in the quintet. Essentially her existence is as active and practically oriented as that of any man. If, as Garrett suggests, she is an American Eve to Jeremiah Catlett's Adam, she is an Eve formed less for submission and "sweet attractive grace" than for survival: from the start, when "her mouth [is] set in that woman's line of wordless resistance" (51), to the end, when she has clearly become the practical head of her family, she lacks the luxury to play the role of helpless dependent.[8] She is in a nearly pure form precisely that part of themselves that many women of subsequent generations will deny or cover over with lace and gentility. It is significant that the independent heroine of the final volume is again named Hannah.

Sally Lacey brings to Beulah the class pride, affected manners, and falsified memory of the East, all of which, like a virus, will strengthen and spread during the ensuing century until they utterly dominate behavior and attitudes. The person who appears least suited to the frontier, paradoxically, will be the one who reshapes it, to the extent that within a generation or two her alien ways will come to seem natural, almost instinctive. Sally's class consciousness, apparent in her advice that "ye can be polite and friendly but 'tis as well to show the lower class of the people right off the ways ye're used to" (244), contains the seeds of the antebellum society portrayed in *Know Nothing*. "All them Cohees, common as dirt, entertained like they was quality," she complains. "To think a daughter of mine should fetch up with such dirt as that" (321–22). Her definition of worth through such objects as English china and lace anticipates the obsessive concern with appearance and material goods in the subsequent novel. Most important, her distortion of her own family and even personal history through memory establishes a dangerous pattern to be followed by succeeding generations. Near the novel's close, her husband worries: "I sometimes think I done her a great wrong, bringin her from what she was used to. But there was nothin there—there was nothin left for us. I've made here what she wanted, but she don't see it. She clings to a dream instead. . . . There ain't a hole deep enough to bury the past. I used to think there was" (325).

Sally Lacey demonstrates the importance of understanding each of these individual novels within the larger context of the quintet. Within *O Beulah Land* itself she might appear, as Nancy Carol Joyner claims, to be "presented as a comic figure" and to be defeated by the environment whose nature she refuses to acknowledge: even her sanity is lost, at the end, when she falls victim to a cruel practical joke.[9] But in light

8. Vance, "History Inherited, History Created," 45; Garrett, *Understanding Mary Lee Settle,* 54.

9. Joyner, "Mary Lee Settle's Connections," 38.

of the culture that evolves through *Know Nothing, The Scapegoat,* and *The Killing Ground,* Sally appears less ridiculous and pathetic than frightening and, in her own way, prescient. Her stone house does get built, her stylish furniture does get purchased, and her mannered, aristocratic society does eventually take hold.

Still, even with the presence of Sally Lacey, *O Beulah Land* is a more hopeful book than *Prisons,* in which the dream of freedom has yet to take shape, or *Know Nothing,* in which it has already begun to be tainted by disillusionment. Jonathan Lacey faces a less harrowing choice than either Johnny Church or Johnny Catlett faces, and he pays in the end a less exorbitant price. Put simply, he alone manages to live beyond early manhood and to imprint on the landscape some version, however imperfect, of his imagined world. The optimism of the novel is largely a reflection of its historical moment; for Lacey, and for many in the society to which he belongs, America is still unambiguously the promised land described in the hymn from which the farm, the novel, and the quintet take their names:

> O Beulah Land, sweet Beulah Land,
> As on thy highest mount I stand,
> I look away across the sea
> Where mansions are prepared for me,
> And view the shining Glory Shore,
> My Heaven, my Home, forevermore.

The open, fertile Virginia frontier seems a fulfillment of a prophecy offered in *Prisons,* where a Parliamentary soldier, dipping into the Bible, reads aloud the passage in Isaiah 62 on which the hymn is based: "Thou shalt no more be termed Forsaken; neither shall thy land any more be termed Desolate: but thou shalt be called Hephzibah, and thy land Beulah: for the Lord delighteth in thee" (85).[10] The seemingly forsaken, desolate Johnny Church is redeemed through the freedom of his descendants.

The tone of the Beulah quintet shifts repeatedly, both subtly within and more broadly among the volumes, so that the story never appears wholly triumphant or wholly despairing. The lines between oppressed

10. A detailed discussion of the significance of the Beulah passage can be found in Dyer, "Taproots History," 34–35. "'Beulah,'" Dyer writes, "means 'Wedded.' The land represents the wedding between the Lord and Hepzibah, the forsaken Israelites."

and oppressor, between the drive for self-sufficiency and dogged possessiveness, are too fine to allow any situation to remain balanced and untainted for long; inevitably, it seems, one person's need will begin to threaten and impinge upon another's. The myth of the promised land is juxtaposed therefore with what Shattuck calls the "counterpart truth" that such land, once gotten, "corrupts as well as inspires."[11] Although there is little hint of corruption at the end of this novel, within a few generations the owners of Beulah will reenact the easy movement from dispossessed to dispossessors first seen in the story of Johnny Church's father. In the ebb and flow of history, the success of Jonathan Lacey is necessary not just to validate the sacrifices of his ancestors but to lay the groundwork for the failures of his children.

*Know Nothing* begins and ends with water. Johnny Catlett virtually enters the novel underwater, tossed at age seven into the Kanawha River to sink or swim. He thrashes, "fighting the river" (7) and his fear of the "big nigger-belly catfish" (5), until he reaches the shore where the slave Minna can cradle him and croon, "Lil old Johnny-cake done licked the river" (7). The scene comes back to him twenty-four years later, as he rides off to fight for Virginia: "He remembered old Telemachus and the nigger-belly catfish. All his life he had been trying to swim away from that great mouth, that hungry jaw, never knowing that he would some day have the energy or even the desire for flight taken from him, and stop struggling, as they said a swimmer did when he was drowning, cease to care with his body" (326). At the novel's end the world is "nothing but rain, sweeping, pounding, never-ending rain" through which the soldiers move "like slow flood water" (334). As insistently as in *Prisons,* the river here represents the current of historical and cultural circumstance into which each individual is placed, sometimes to be carried passively along, sometimes, like Johnny Church, to struggle, sometimes to drown. How Johnny Catlett, along with the family whose head he eventually becomes, moves inexorably from swimming to drowning, from insistence on survival to acquiescence in destruction, is the story at the heart of the novel.

Unlike *Prisons* and *The Scapegoat,* whose historical locations are likely

11. Shattuck, Introduction, xi.

to seem relatively unfamiliar, *Know Nothing* is set in the most frequently re-created period in American history. In writing about the South during the years leading up to the Civil War, Settle ran the risk of being lumped together with the many writers of historical romance and of being accused, as she was, of aiming at "those voracious readers . . . who have never got over *Gone with the Wind*."[12] Certainly all the trappings are present, from the plantation to the genteel watering place and from the spoiled southern belle to the black mammy. Certainly, too, there are signs that she had widely known historical images in mind when creating the world of *Know Nothing*. Her aim, however, was not to emulate but to undermine; the vision of the South presented in the novel is intended as a corrective to the distorted vision created and reinforced by popular retellings of history. Because the antebellum South is among the most dangerously mythologized of all historical eras, *Know Nothing* is the most emphatically antimythological novel in the quintet. And because the truth of the period is so often obscured, Settle is more than usually concerned with the precise, detailed representation of social and political movements. This novel is the easiest of the five to read as comprehensive history.

In the years between the end of *O Beulah Land* and the start of *Know Nothing,* from 1774 to 1837, the Beulah settlement has matured into a sprawling plantation, complete with a "new white-painted brick house" (58), which is filled with "all the latest thing" (59), a travelers' inn, and dozens of inhabitants. Among the more prominent additions are a profitable salt mine and, problematically, slavery, an institution about which the family from the start has mixed feelings. Matters of class and blood are even more important here than in *O Beulah Land,* though ironically the social and familial divisions of the earlier novel are now barely discernible. Peregrine Catlett, present owner of the plantation, is the great-grandson of both Jonathan Lacey and Jeremiah Catlett, and his wife Leah is a descendant of the Cutwrights, among the less reputable of the settlement's original tenants. Another great-grandson, Brandon Lacey, has married a Sally Crawford to produce, in more ways than one, another Sally Lacey. Even many of the slaves descend illegitimately from Jonathan Lacey or one of his heirs. Virtually every character in

12. Hart, Review of *Know Nothing,* 3105.

the novel is somehow connected to every other by blood, marriage, or illicit coupling.

The pace of *Know Nothing* reflects the characters' perception that a world apparently frozen in time is becoming increasingly subject to change and outside influence. Book One lingers over two days in July of 1837; Books Two and Three quicken to cover, respectively, three months and five years. Superficially the most tranquil section of the novel, the first book introduces the forces that threaten and will eventually undermine the apparently stable social order. Brandon and Sally Lacey, polished, well-dressed, and broke, travel west to Beulah to beg money from the Catletts, whose own appearance of wealth is somewhat deceiving and who are therefore unable to help. Annie Catlett, Peregrine's spinster sister, is carrying on an affair with Big Dan O'Neill, an Irish laborer, beginning a process that will intertwine and, within only a few decades, reverse the fortunes of the two families. Methodist Leah Catlett and her elder son Lewis are morally opposed to the slavery that maintains their way of life, and for Lewis this opposition is mingled with an intense Oedipal hatred of his father: "It was terrible to see your father's sins all around you, black, ungrateful, taking everything" (93). Most ominously, the two most sensitive characters introduced, the children Melinda Lacey and Johnny Catlett, seem subtly alienated from the family and culture around them, she as a poor relation and he as a favored son unsure of his ability to play the expected roles. Especially Johnny appears trapped between the desire to "make everybody else leave him alone" (84) and the belief, enforced by his mother, "that disobedient children, unless they repent, come to a bad end, and that there is no blessing on such as do not honor their parents and respect them" (89).

Twelve years later, in Book Two, the family converges on the fashionable spa at Egeria Springs to escape the cholera epidemic terrifying the entire river valley. The habits of southern society seem exaggerated at Egeria, a mannered and rigidly hierarchical place combining the formality of Bath with the studied flamboyance of Camelot. Melinda comes there hoping to renew her romance with Johnny, who has been away at college, but he seems standoffish and ill at ease, unable yet to commit to the permanent relationship she desires. Unintentionally Melinda attracts, then intentionally enthralls, yet another cousin, the immensely wealthy Crawford Kregg. Few of the other family members, meanwhile, seem comfortable. Peregrine Catlett frets about Beulah and about a southern culture that is, in the words of one character, "committing suicide" (148); Sally Lacey, now widowed, is distraught at her inability to marry off her plain daughter; Lewis Catlett finds in fundamentalist Christianity added strength for his hatred of both slavery and his father. The book ends with the announced engagement of Crawford and Melinda and the decision by Johnny to leave behind disappointment and responsibility and journey to California.

An image recurrent throughout the novel's first two books embodies at least one of the problems in all of this strained, self-conscious behavior. Melinda and the young slave Toey are initially described as gazing into a pool "with the objective contemplation of women at a mirror, coolly judging their reflections in the water" (46). Thereafter, mirrors appear to be hanging in nearly everyone's room, contemplating perpetually the actions of the characters: Sally Lacey watches "the dignity of her own movements in the long mirror" (59); Annie Catlett stares at "herself in the dresser mirror" (64); Lewis Catlett pauses "just long enough to look at himself in the mirror" (95); Lydia Catlett arranges "the pier-glass so that she [can] glance at herself on first rising up from her pillow" (119); Melinda sighs before Crawford "as carefully as if she were practicing before her mirror in the morning" (154); Mr. Wellington Smythe, an Egeria dandy, turns reluctantly from "the safety of his mirror" (169). The clue to understanding the mirror's significance is provided in a description of Crawford, who, in allowing himself to be seduced by Melinda, "once again . . . faced the expected and bowed to his fate, acquiescent to his image of himself" (153). Most of the characters in this novel have created images of themselves to which they continually acquiesce, acting less out of honesty or desire than out of a sense of what is expected, telling themselves, in effect, "this is the way a person of *my* sort should behave." Melinda has from the start constructed an image of herself as "a proud, aloof orphaned heroine" (153), and she will remain in character to the end, regardless of reality or the consequences of her role playing; Johnny is so constrained by his role as a southern gentleman's son that he flees rather than violate its expected codes of behavior. A society of this nature is maddeningly resistant to change, since an individual stepping outside his defined role would feel as guilty as an actor who knowingly alters his lines.

Book Three opens in 1856 in St. Jo, Missouri, where Johnny has landed as county clerk after returning east from California. Clearly he is a "man to whom something [has] happened which [has] stripped him of the old pose" (249): the graceful boy has become a participant in the bloody Kansas wars and appears worn down by the brutality of his environment and his own protracted rootlessness. Finally he returns to Beulah, to find his father dying and the family anxious to burden him with precisely those responsibilities he had attempted seven years earlier to flee. The narrative then rushes through the next five years, during which Johnny attempts to remain upright in a collapsing world: Melinda dies, having borne a child conceived during a brief, illicit relationship with Johnny; Beulah slowly fails as wealth shifts to cities where, as his brother-in-law informs him, people "don't like what you stand fer" (311); Virginia votes to secede and Johnny goes to war knowing his abolitionist brother will be fighting on the other side. At the end, carried along by the flood of panicked soldiers, he appears utterly to have lost the freedom to choose a position or direction.

The Know Nothing party becomes an important emblem in Book Three of the corrosive blindness and insularity of the South. This nativist, anti-Catholic political party, so called because "all members professed ignorance of the party and were instructed to reply 'I don't know' to all questions," gained rapid popularity in the South around the time of the 1856 elections. W. Darrell Overdyke explains how southern party members perceived people in other parts of the country: "There was little doubt in the minds of the Southern Know-Nothings that the three and a half million Europeans who were pouring into Michigan, Wisconsin, Minnesota, Iowa, Ohio, Indiana, and Illinois meant ill to the South. Basically antagonistic toward slavery, in favor of personal liberty and small farms, foreigners went into the Democratic and Republican parties in great numbers." The Know Nothing party's greatest success actually came in the Northeast, where it nearly won New York in the 1854 elections and did win Massachusetts and Delaware. The issue of slavery soon split the party in the South, with the antislavery members leaving to join the newly formed Republican party.[13] More important for Settle than the specific platforms of this

13. W. Darrell Overdyke, *The Know-Nothing Party in the South* (Baton Rouge, 1950), 44, 198, 57–72, 198–210.

extremely factionalized movement, though, is its demonstration of the ease with which idealism and regional pride degenerate into oversimplification and bigotry. Dan Neill gives this diagnosis of the attitude in the area around Beulah: "Folks hereabouts are damn sick of talkin rum and niggers. They don't want no foreigners. They don't hanker after no black Catholics risen up to kill all the Protestants" (266). "Know Nothings," complains Peregrine Catlett. "By God, ain't nobody been better named" (268). Ultimately the party name broadens to describe all deliberately chosen ignorance and passivity, as Johnny wonders "if it was only he, and men like him, who were fated to be the know nothings, to question, to see beyond their attitudes, but not to speak" (334).

Each novel in the quintet, it should by now be clear, brings a measure of individuality to the larger unity of the whole. *Know Nothing* is the most tragic of the novels, in the sense that it centers on a mistaken choice whose consequences are terrible and far-reaching. Both Johnny Church and Jonathan Lacey choose conscience over loyalty to authority, and from a historical perspective those decisions appear not just admirable but wise: Church and those like him prepare the ground for American democracy, and Lacey hastens the expansion of the country westward. Faced with a comparable decision, Settle acknowledges, "Johnny Catlett fails," for "he doesn't pay the price of freedom" (Appendix B, p. 164). Because "his mother's moist heart-broken blackmailing eyes" and the "quiet face of his father frozen with anger" (240) overwhelm his knowledge and belief, Johnny remains self-destructively loyal to family and region and enacts, in small, the origin of the Civil War. His special curse is to understand his mistake as he is committing it. The image of Charles McAndrews, a southerner with "some integrity inside him—conscience, God" (252) more powerful than loyalty, haunts him, and near the end he recognizes that there "was something he missed somewhere along the way, some time of decision; he searched back in his mind for it like a lost thing, a lost moment, but he could not find it" (304). In his defense, his situation does seem considerably more difficult than those of his ancestors: unlike Lacey and especially Church, who face clear moments of decision when issues crystallize and define themselves, this Johnny actually faces a lifetime of scarcely noticed choices whose consequences are difficult to predict but whose cumulative effect is crushing.

Although *Know Nothing* focuses on the same struggle between authority and freedom, between Creon and Antigone, as the other volumes, it devotes more time and appears to grant more sympathy to the side of authority. "In one sense," Garrett contends, "*Know Nothing* might be seen in part as Creon's side of the story."[14] Without being an apology for slave owners, the novel manages to demonstrate how even good men may end by defending bad behavior and how the exercise of power may become more burdensome than pleasurable. Peregrine and Johnny Catlett are in some ways as limited and isolated by their positions of patriarchal authority as are the slaves and women they control. The older man in particular is an oddly melancholic figure, troubled by the "thousand pinpricks of demand" that have forced an apparently gentle being to clothe himself in "the armor of lord and master," as he thinks "of how lonely God must be sometimes, with the judgments demanded of Him, but with no one to turn to to be judged" (65). When a slave tells Johnny, "You ain't got no more freedom than we got" (238), the familiar theme of the interrelatedness of master and servant is taken to a new level. Whereas in the earlier novels Settle explores the ease with which the same individual can occupy positions of dominance and subservience, here she suggests, I think, that the differences between the positions may be partly illusory and that the ruler may become as entrapped as those he rules. In a paradoxical sense, the victimizer may be less free than the victim, for while the former becomes *wholly* the role he plays, the latter is a victim but something more. The slave chides and taunts Johnny with this truth: "It's you got the burden. We got ways. Live a whole life in secret, then play nigger" (237–38).

The force of smothering, protective authority has stunted the nature of the slaves, obviously, but also the nature of the southern women, who are seen by masters like Peregrine Catlett as the white man's other burden: "Women and niggers. They ain't fitten to look after theirselves" (269). One of the more subtle tragedies of southern society, *Know Nothing* suggests, has been the domestication and distortion of the female personality under the weight of custom and expectation. Hannah Bridewell, tough and pragmatic, has been literally and figuratively for-

14. Garrett, *Understanding Mary Lee Settle,* 63.

gotten, while the spoiled nature of Sally Lacey has been nurtured and encouraged, to be reborn in an even more stultifying form in her descendants. This novel's Sally Lacey is a debased version of the first, all manners and vanity with little underlying strength, but she is also as much a product of southern culture as is cotton or tobacco. When Settle writes that "Sally's carefully modulated genteel voice, which carried in it the capability of nervous screaming, had slipped into that perpetual discussion of rules and personalities which passed for conversation when two or three Virginia ladies were gathered together" (142), she defines the two dominant characteristics of the southern gentlewoman of this age, repression of feeling and obsession with apparently trivial forms and details. The voice is "carefully modulated," or controlled, and "genteel," or proper, but it masks a current of nearly hysterical emotion; it discusses not ideas or events or even domestic arrangements but "rules and personalities." Southern women, like southern men, are trapped within prescribed roles, but because their roles are more passive and limited in scope than men's, their need for denial and self-control is greater. From earliest childhood the girls at Beulah feel constrained by Leah Catlett, "pacing the house on the winter nights, watching, checking, owning" (284), and Leah herself feels watched and owned in turn. Even Melinda, the closest thing to a free-spirited woman in the novel, eventually feels "all the unthinking demands and blood relationships on her shoulders" and wonders "if this was what was called defeat" (282). The trivial is invested with great importance because so much that is truly important is rigorously excluded from female experience, and "all the great force of life had to be concentrated on details too small to hold it" (27). Once again, however, in another blurring of distinctions between the empowered and the powerless, it becomes difficult to tell if the women are more controlled or controlling: the innocence of Sally Lacey and her like is a "demanding innocence" (13), and the men are forever struggling to satisfy a dependency they have themselves created and encouraged.

Whatever their differences, the men and women in *Know Nothing* are ultimately united in their willful blindness. At the core of this novel named for ignorance is the study both of a whole society devoted to the denial and distortion of truth and, in an even broader sense, of the many ways truth may be buried beneath the language and traditions of a culture. Confronted by a crumbling, empty system and a history whose lessons are inconsistent with their images of themselves, repeatedly these characters romanticize the present and mythologize the past. In *Know Nothing,* writes William Schafer, "we find . . . that Mark Twain's deep suspicion of Sir Walter Scott was well-founded—perhaps Scott *did* cause the Civil War."[15] This is exaggeration, of course, but the chivalric vocabulary of Scott and others had, by the mid-nineteenth century, crept into the language of the American South and had encouraged the construction of an elaborate fantasy world. It seems innocuous enough for young men unselfconsciously to call themselves Sir Launcelot of Tuckahoe Springs or Wilfred of Ivanhoe and to participate in jousting tournaments, but along with the costumes and ceremonies comes a tendency to cast oneself as a character in a romance and to act as if life will assume the shape of a novelistic plot. Johnny Catlett and Melinda Lacey and Crawford Kregg see themselves as like "the Knights of Old" (9) or "the queen of far Araby" (47) or "Sir Galahad" (139) and are caught by surprise when uncooperative circumstances prevent them from playing the expected roles. Settle always becomes suspicious, moreover, when the connections between language and meaning are deliberately weakened and when the natural evolution of a language through history is artificially distorted. No word is by itself good or bad or precisely or imprecisely expressive, but in this context these words are inappropriate, resulting in absurdities like Melinda's "You ain't nothing but my minion, arrant knave" (47).

As imagination and desire transform the present into a romance, communal memory transforms the past into a myth or fairy tale whose happy ending is the current moment. Melinda's recitation to Toey of her personal history is a child's version of the "repression of family facts" that seems to come naturally to the Laceys and Catletts:[16]

> "Now I'll tell you about the funeral," she said through the apple. "Once upon a time . . ."
>
> "This wasn't no story. This was real," Toey broke in.
>
> "You just shut your mouth. Whose funeral was this anyhow?"
>
> Toey shut up. She was afraid Melinda wouldn't tell.
>
> "Once upon a time, there was this great Injun fighter and glorious hero

15. Schafer, "History Darkly," 82.
16. Vance, "History Inherited, History Created," 48.

> of the Revolution," Melinda went on comfortably. "He lived in a big palace in the West with his dear little granddaughter, who he loved more than life itself."
>
> "You forgot the daddy," Toey reminded her.
>
> "He died a hero's death."
>
> "Who was the dear little granddaughter?" Toey prompted on.
>
> Melinda put her arm around Toey. It still felt wet and cold.
>
> "That was me," she yearned, making up details as she went along. (51)

This exchange is among the most definitive in the quintet. Toey recognizes immediately the power of language to shape one's understanding of events: the formulaic "Once upon a time" guarantees that the narrative will assume the shape not of the "real" but of a "story" and that the storyteller, freed from the constraints of reality, will shape and edit details to meet the demands of plot. The recitation is less history than litany, with Toey playing the part of respondent ("Who was the dear little granddaughter?") and appreciative audience. The pleasure in the listener arises not from the prolongation of suspense, since she already knows the outcome of the story, but from the gratification of expectation, though there is a certain amount of curiosity about the embellishments Melinda will add to this telling of the tale. Melinda is herself a "yearn[ing]" narrator, guided by what she wishes, not what she knows, to have happened. She is also, in miniature, the quintessential American historian of the first half of the nineteenth century, participating in what Clark identifies as "a tradition of thought in the United States which would rather dispense with objective history" in favor of myth.[17] Even her cliches, "loved more than life itself" and "died a hero's death," are the literary staples of the time.

Melinda's story points, additionally, to the special dependence of *Know Nothing* on *O Beulah Land*. Only the reader of the earlier novel could know that Peregrine Lacey, here "great Injun fighter and glorious hero of the Revolution," was in fact a "blood crazy" loner, "drunk with killin'" (351), who was disinherited by his horrified father. Again and again, the reader of *Know Nothing*, privileged by a more accurate and immediate knowledge of the characters' histories than they themselves possess, is struck by the irony of their ignorance and distortion. Jeremiah Catlett and Hannah Bridewell, indentured servant and trans-

17. Clark, *History, Ideology, and Myth,* 46.

ported thief, are recast by a later generation as European nobility: "The Catletts now . . . were French. Norman French knights. Their name was really de Chatelet, which means castle. They laid claim to Beulah with a ruby ring and a silver riding crop. It shows what fine folks they were to have such things" (74). The ruby was found by Hannah as she wandered in the Endless Mountains, surviving on raw squirrel and bear meat; the riding crop was stolen from a dead ensign by Squire Raglan and from him in turn by Jeremiah. Later the ruins of the Catlett cabin will be misidentified as an "ancient hearth" (154) and Raglan's grave as belonging to an "Indian princess" and her heroic lover (188). This mythologizing becomes menacing when it moves beyond self-glorification and begins to pervert the ideals on which Beulah and the country were founded. When anti-Catholic, anti-immigrant Crawford Kregg insists that "our forebears came here for freedom, not because they couldn't make a living, or were the spawn of foreign jails" (266), he gets his own history exactly wrong and destroys a potentially unifying bond with those reenacting that history in the present. The point of all this is not merely that the mythologizing of history is bad but that it is as difficult to prevent as the gradual erosion of personal memory: because tossing away the remnants of the past as "battered junk" (297) is easier than reconstructing their actual significance, those seeking to escape the myth are often condemned, as the narrator says in *The Clam Shell,* to "dry pastlessness" (172).

By themselves, *O Beulah Land* and *Know Nothing* appear to trace a gradual downward path. Although there are triumphs, especially in the second half of *O Beulah Land,* and though moments of heroism and insight dot the entire narrative, the general movement is toward disillusionment and the corruption of ideals. The story that begins with Hannah Bridewell's frantic struggle for survival ends with her great-great-grandson Johnny Catlett's act of suicidal passivity: at the start of *O Beulah Land* she refuses to surrender to "the law which is so inevitable that it can crush the will and mind of a man" (5); at the close of *Know Nothing* he "stop[s] struggling, as they said a swimmer did when he was drowning, cease[s] to care with his body" (326). The mystery explored by these novels is how the first attitude, which Settle sees as responsible for the American Revolution and the establishment of the

United States, managed to decay within a century into the second, which she sees as responsible for the Civil War. In answer, she points to a complex group of interrelated, nearly inevitable, but nonetheless tragic developments. The tendency of personal, familial, and communal memory is to mythologize the past, covering over the truth with a veneer of bias and desire; the tendency of the oppressed when granted power is to become oppressors themselves; the tendency of ownership, of the attainment of the promised land, is, as Shattuck says, to "stifle ideals and promises."[18] Because, for the early generations of Americans, the past was so sordid, the background of oppression so widespread, and the image of the promised land so powerful, the subsequent urge to mythologize, oppress, and claim ownership was especially strong. And because history teaches the seductive danger of these impulses, the study of the past is, for Settle, indispensable.

It becomes easy to see, in retrospect, why the demand for further volumes was implicit from the beginning in *O Beulah Land* and *Know Nothing*. Placed into the broader context of the quintet, their movement appears considerably less disheartening, not so much a story of disintegration as a down period in a larger cyclic progression. *O Beulah Land* becomes the upward surge following the apparent defeat of Johnny Church in *Prisons*. *Know Nothing* is the apocalyptic tumult prior to the social reordering of *The Scapegoat* and *The Killing Ground*. The balance between "dry pastlessness" and the "singing insistence of the blood" (*Clam Shell,* 172), between "the unblessings of our fathers" (*Prisons,* 67) and "imperial love" (*Know Nothing,* 292), between Antigone and Creon, tilts first in one direction, then the other. The precise terms of the confrontation change, but its essential nature remains, as it must, unaltered, for the temporary victory of one side or the other does not free subsequent generations from having to make for themselves the same decisions and sacrifices. The question of whether there can be any fundamental changes in this cyclic or oscillating movement remains unaddressed until the final volume, where it becomes clear that the quintet is itself a means of subtly altering the conflict it repeatedly dramatizes.

18. Shattuck, Introduction, xi.

# *The Scapegoat* Watching a Lie Begin 5

Upon its publication in 1980, *The Scapegoat* was greeted by a more enthusiastic initial response than was given any other novel in the quintet. Writing on the front page of the *New York Times Book Review,* E. L. Doctorow praised Settle's "impressive" powers of description, her "authoritative" knowledge of her subject, and her "palpable instinct" for panorama and high drama. Robert Houston, as I noted earlier, called *The Scapegoat* "as good a novel as anyone writing in this country today could have written," and Rosellen Brown dismissed the novel's flaws as "amount[ing] to little in this absorbing and ambitious book." George Garrett immediately characterized the novel as "stronger, more daring, and an even more impressive example of graceful virtuosity" than her earlier work. And Malcolm Cowley, from the beginning one of Settle's most vocal supporters, called *The Scapegoat* "the most humanly complicated of all her books."[1] In part, this flood of enthusiasm can be attributed to the fact that her previous novel, *Blood Tie,* won the National Book Award, transforming her into one of those writers expected to

1. See Doctorow, Review of *The Scapegoat,* 1; Houston, Review of *The Scapegoat,* 469; Rosellen Brown, Review of *The Scapegoat,* in *New Republic,* December 27, 1980, p. 37; and Garrett, "Mary Lee Settle," 287. Cowley's remarks are quoted on the dust jacket of the original hardcover edition of *The Scapegoat* (New York, 1980). As early as 1965, Granville Hicks thanked Cowley in print for "calling Miss Settle's work to [his] attention" (Granville Hicks, Foreword to *O Beulah Land* [New York, 1965], xiii).

publish important books. In part, however, it can be attributed to the nature of *The Scapegoat* itself, which seems better suited to appeal to a contemporary audience—or at least to that part of the audience given to reviewing and criticizing literature—than any of its predecessors in the quintet. The novel's setting and subject, a West Virginia coal miners' strike in 1912, unlike those of *O Beulah Land* and *Know Nothing,* are not the stuff of historical romance and invite no denigrating comparisons. Although historical in a broad sense, moreover, they are not lodged so deeply in the past as to seem quaint or escapist. The novel's style and structure are decidedly modern: its narrative is Settle's most fragmented and complex, its plot, her least conventional, its chorus of voices, her most diverse and linguistically distinctive. Even the novel's increased absorption with the working class and immigrant cultures (no cavaliers or plantation owners here) would tend to increase its appeal to contemporary highbrow sensibilities. *The Scapegoat* is apt to be likened more to the proletarian novel or Faulkner than to the popular romance or *Gone with the Wind.*

In technique, at least, *The Scapegoat* is an outgrowth as much of its immediate predecessor as of *Know Nothing* or *Prisons. Blood Tie,* published in 1978, traces the interactions among a group of people living or vacationing on the Turkish coast, and the diversity and relative strangeness of the subject seem to have forced Settle to adapt her usual approaches to character and narrative. Because the variations among the characters are more substantial and the geographic and cultural setting more enigmatic than in her previous fiction, the presentation of a balanced, comprehensible picture becomes more complex. The usual narrative fragmentation is intensified as differences in viewpoint, language, and background become more extreme. The central consciousness may shift within a few pages from a Turkish boy to a British homosexual to an American former accountant, the location, from the sea floor to an archaeological dig. No character is granted the central, privileged position of a Jonathan Lacey or Johnny Catlett, so truth becomes even more decidedly an amalgam of individually limited points of view. What keeps the kaleidoscopic narrative from breaking apart, aside from the interweaving of its various plots, is the consistent precision and lucidity of the prose.

*The Scapegoat,* "complex in its own terms as well as in relation to the rest of the quintet," is structurally and stylistically a more intricate version of *Blood Tie*.[2] In roughly three hundred pages the novel presents nearly three dozen characters, at least a half-dozen of whom can with some justification be assigned the story's central position. The cultural and ethnic diversity among these characters is greater than in any of the other Beulah novels: joining the familiar Laceys and Catletts are rustic poor from the West Virginia mountains, Italian mine workers, English and Scottish administrators, and Polish, Jewish, and French strikebreakers. Men and women educated at Princeton and Vassar interact with others unable to read or speak English. The reader's awareness of this diversity is heightened by the novel's radically fragmented point of view, which shifts continually among various levels of omniscience, among various degrees of proximity to the central action, and even, on occasion, from third to first person and past to present tense. Eighteen different characters serve at least once as the narrative's central consciousness or the viewpoint through which the third-person voice is filtered; three serve as first-person narrators; sixty-three times, by my count, the narrative shifts among these viewpoints and the more comprehensive perspective of the authorial persona. *The Scapegoat* is comprised less of a story or series of events than of a set of simultaneous, overlapping, but subtly different stories, none of which has any special claim to accuracy or reliability.

Difficulties arise in this narrative not because events are partially glimpsed but because they are glimpsed repeatedly from dissimilar and sometimes contradictory perspectives. Mary Rose Lacey, for example, narrator of the novel's opening pages, describes a consequential meeting as taking place on the afternoon of Friday, June 7, 1912; later her sister Althea claims that "Mary Rose has rearranged her whole puny little past to suit herself" (145) and that the meeting took place in May. Shortly after Mary Rose recalls herself lingering defiantly on the lawn, the third-person narrator adds that "what Mary Rose did not remember was that when she stood alone in the grass she was crying and she was afraid to go too near her mother" (25). Even more common than these differences in fact are differences in opinion, judgment, and emotional response. Again and again, what appears tragic to one character appears

2. Garrett, *Understanding Mary Lee Settle,* 63.

ludicrous to another, what seems outrageous to one seems morally justified to the next, and so on. In the absence of an authoritative central voice, the reader is forced to extract from these conflicting perspectives the actual meaning and tone of the novel's events.

What Settle is attempting here should by now be relatively clear. As in *O Beulah Land* and *Know Nothing,* she is seeking to avoid the limitations of personal vision and the distortions of memory by re-creating the past from as many different perspectives as possible, assembling a complete, or at least reliable, picture from a series of partial ones. If, as Hayden White argues, "every fully realized story . . . endows events, whether real or imaginary, with a significance they do not possess as a mere sequence," then perhaps a series of overlapping stories will more nearly approach the actuality of the events themselves.[3] *The Scapegoat* is more radically fragmented than the earlier novels, however, and appears to carry different epistemological implications. In *O Beulah Land* and *Know Nothing,* where a central narrative voice is in control and where some perspectives appear clearly more reliable than others, truth seems elusive, hidden beneath layers of memory and myth, but ultimately discoverable; the reader, granted a comprehensive and historically distanced view, may arrive at a deeper understanding of events than any of the individual characters has. In *The Scapegoat* the suggestion seems to be that truth, as it is commonly conceived of, may not exist. No single version of events, that is, not even one pieced together from a collection of partial versions, can ever claim to be truer than other, different versions that might be pieced together by other readers or historians. The one doing the piecing together, after all, is limited in so doing by his or her own partiality. The externals (names, dates, places) may be authoritatively determined but not the significance that underlies them.

It might appear that, twenty-four years into the writing of the quintet, Settle had lost faith in the validity of the enterprise: for the historical novelist, no insight would be potentially more disturbing than that truth is in the end indeterminate. I believe, though, that this alteration in perspective strengthened her belief in the importance of historical fiction, or at least in historical fiction of the particular kind she embraces in *The Scapegoat* and *The Killing Ground.* Certainly, her most

3. White, *Content of the Form,* 14.

emphatic defenses of the form have come since the publication of those two novels. If historical truth must finally be an individual determination, then the best historian—the most useful historian—is one who puts the reader in a position to make such a determination. A single narrative, selected and arranged from a single perspective, would seem less helpful than a collection of narratives out of which the reader might construct a coherent version of the past. The writer of historical fiction has more "freedom" (Appendix B, p. 158) than the writer of ostensibly nonfictional history to create and investigate the chorus of voices brought together in a novel such as *The Scapegoat,* less need to assert the ultimate authority of a single, controlling voice. Whereas the historian, implicitly or explicitly, lays claim to a privileged position in the selection and interpretation of events, the novelist roaming from viewpoint to viewpoint avoids (or disguises) such a claim. The truthfulness of this latter kind of historical narrative lies, paradoxically, in its refusal to insist on its own special access to the truth.

These multiple perspectives are woven together in *The Scapegoat* into a narrative whose movement through present time is interrupted, sometimes for long periods, by shifts into the past and future. Extended flashbacks are a favorite device of Settle's (they comprise, for instance, a substantial portion of *Prisons*) and are used here to explore the backgrounds that have given rise to the viewpoints of individual characters. Ways of apprehending the present, that is, are repeatedly seen as products of personal and cultural history. Less conventional is the use of what Garrett calls "flash forwards," leaps as far as fifteen years into the future that reveal not only the eventual outcome of the ongoing drama but radical changes in the fortunes of families and of the region itself.[4] By eliminating a certain amount of suspense, these flash forwards create a momentary Brechtian alienation effect, muting the emotions and thereby objectifying the reader's response to a potentially tragic sequence of events. They also generate a host of ironies, as when one learns that Mary Rose, a "pretty little thing" at fifteen, will turn into a librarian who "has two shirtwaists and looks like a picked chicken" (145) or that Neville Roundtree, filled with plans for the future, will be killed in the Battle of the Somme. Their most important purpose,

4. Garrett, *Understanding Mary Lee Settle,* 66.

however, seems to be to reveal memory at work: before the action is even completed, one learns how it will appear in the future under the distorting influence of prejudice, resentment, and desire. Or rather, one learns that the action will be transformed in the future into a variety of different actions. Dan Neill, for example, one of the central figures in the plot, is recalled by Mary Rose a year after the events of June, 1912, as having been "desperately lonely and misunderstood" (7); by Lily four years later as a "war-lover" (189); by Althea fifteen years later as "our white hope" (153); and by Mooney McKarkle at some unspecified future time as "a gentleman to his fingertips" (174). Drunk and fifteen years removed from events, Althea confesses that she remembers "everything from her own pointaview" but doubtless speaks for Settle when she adds, "Well who the hell doesn't?" (146).

Binding together these disparate viewpoints and time frames is prose both dramatically variable, in diction, complexity of syntax, and so on, and consistently different from the prose in Settle's earlier work. The nature of this difference is subtle but, for the reader of the entire quintet, distinct. The characteristic Settle voice that speaks loudly in *O Beulah Land* and *Know Nothing* and that can be heard clearly within the monologue of Johnny Church is more muted in *The Scapegoat,* where it is submerged beneath the individualized voices of the many central characters. The relations between the characters and the language in which they are described are in this novel more immediate, generating prose that is slightly more fluid and impressionistic, as if the prologue of *O Beulah Land,* infused with the consciousness of Hannah Bridewell, had been extended over three hundred pages. This results in, among other things, Settle's most widespread use of the vernacular, which in *O Beulah Land* and *Know Nothing* had been confined largely to dialogue and in *Prisons* had been limited by Johnny Church's Oxford education. Here, the vernacular can be heard not just in spoken language but in the first-person monologues of Mary Rose and Althea and in the many internal comments and reflections spread throughout the third-person narrative. None of the following passages is part of the novel's dialogue, yet each exemplifies a slightly different version of West Virginia discourse:

> Holy cow, it was some punkins! Masculine punkins, not feminine punkins. There weren't any frills. There didn't need to be, just a deep Turkey

> carpet all over what he called the observation room, and those real deep punched leather chairs that look like they're stuffed with money. (17)

> I didn't give a shit about the strike. I thought it's brought me Anderson. Later it was a different story, I'll tell the world. It ruined Papa and it was the ruination of me, but then that evening I just lay in the hammock and waited. (148)

> What you wanted to do was you wanted to give them something to do. Shit fire, she ought to know—make it more like a strike and less like a goddamn picnic. (53)

> Seems to me there's always been some damned woman with wet eyes watching me and waiting for me to say it, whatever it is they want to hear. God almighty my hand looks like it's made out of paper. (37)

> Ann Eldridge wouldn't of been there if it hadn't of been for Mr. Godley. Essie had been stuck there a year when Ann Eldridge married Beverley and she was never so glad to see anybody in all her born days. (48)

> Another thing. That day was different. He almost didn't get away because of Carlo Michele. Everybody was performing for Carlo Michele. Oh boy. Mama was one new lady. (95)

Given that *The Scapegoat* is the first novel in the quintet to include characters who might have lived during Settle's own lifetime, this familiarity with the spoken language of the region is not surprising. Rather than re-creating through historic memory the vocabulary, diction, and syntax of the past, she is here retrieving from personal memory the language of her own "parents and their contemporaries, who still had habits of speech from the days when they were growing up before World War I."[5] Small differences—differences between "shit" and "shit fire" or "goddamn" and "God almighty"—define the ethnic and social divisions of the limited world within which the events of the novel occur.

The main action of *The Scapegoat* takes place within the seventeen hours between three o'clock in the afternoon on Friday, June 7, 1912, and eight o'clock the following morning. Although its setting is the familiar Kanawha valley just across the river from the Beulah planta-

5. Settle, "Recapturing the Past," 37.

tion, the landscape bears little resemblance to the one last glimpsed in *Know Nothing*. Coal mining has replaced agriculture as the area's dominant industry; farmers have come out of the West Virginia hills to join immigrants, mostly Italian, in populating the mining village of Lacey Creek (demonstrating the futility of the anti-immigrant Know Nothing movement in the previous novel). The town of Canona has grown into a medium-sized city, and the railroad has connected the entire region to a sprawling urban-industrial network. For this generation of Laceys, Catletts, and Neills, the historical changes have not proven especially beneficial. Beverley Lacey, descendant of *O Beulah Land*'s Jonathan, is being forced from his coal mine by corporate pressure, and Jake Catlett, son of Lewis, nephew of Johnny, is a miner living in the cabin to which his abolitionist father had been banished. Lewis dies "grasping that old whip with the silver handle" (47), Squire Raglan's whip, previously an emblem of family continuity. "Afterwards they had to pry it loose and Jake took and made a carving knife out of it," for "the whip part by that time looked like a sick rat's tail" (47). Princeton-educated Dan Neill, grandson of *Know Nothing*'s Little Dan O'Neill, works as a hired gun for the mining companies, his expectations of wealth having been frustrated five years before: "Captain Neill's granddaddy, Senator Neill, lost his shirt in the Tennessee Coal and Land Company in 1907 and after that his father shot himself in the garden across the river at Beulah" (8). If the plantation first envisioned by Jonathan Lacey has since the eighteenth century represented the Promised Land, these descendants of its founders are in exile. Once again, the dispossessors have become the dispossessed.

The series of novels that forms the quintet, it should be emphasized, conveys the passage of time differently, and perhaps more powerfully, than would a single, long, multigenerational novel. Change here is apprehended in two ways simultaneously: within the novels themselves as a gradual, sometimes imperceptible process; among the novels together as a rapid sequence of abrupt and momentous alterations. Few single novels could present the striking temporal juxtapositions of this group of novels, as when Dan Neill's father, last seen wetting his pants in *Know Nothing,* is alluded to as a suicide in *The Scapegoat* or when Toey, Melinda's slave and companion in the earlier novel, is presented as an ancient matriarch in the latter. A novel of three hundred pages focused on a single day, *The Scapegoat* yet manages, because of its place in the larger structure, to demonstrate the rapidity of historical change, which suggests, again, the importance of reading the volumes together and in sequence.

Like *Prisons, The Scapegoat* draws heavily on documentary evidence, extrapolating from established facts and weaving together actual and fictional characters and incidents. April 1, 1912, marked the expiration of a contract between the United Mine Workers (UMW) and the Kanawha field operators and the beginning of what Dale Fetherling calls the "worst coal war" in West Virginia history. For more than a year, eruptions of violence in the area of Paint Creek (called Lacey Creek in the novel) would result in scores of deaths, cessations in production, damage to property, and impassioned political and economic battles within the state. That militiamen, sent to the area in September of 1912, managed to confiscate "1,872 rifles, 556 pistols, 6 machine guns, 225,000 rounds of ammunition, 480 blackjacks, as well as daggers, bayonets, and brass knuckles from the two sides" and that for months civil liberties in the region of the strike were virtually suspended suggest the dimensions of the conflict. What must have drawn Settle to the dispute was its seminal nature, its status as a "pitch point" that signaled a dramatic shift in historical currents: by the time it ended in July of 1913, UMW membership had increased from two thousand to five thousand and by the end of World War I, about half of West Virginia's mines would be unionized.[6] The existence of a long Senate investigation into the strikes, containing thousands of pages of verbatim testimony, must also have seemed a tempting factual and stylistic foundation on which to construct a novel.[7]

In June of 1912, when *The Scapegoat* is set, the confrontation between miners and hired guns was still in its preliminary stages, the violence more potential than actual. The seventeen-hour period on which the novel focuses climaxes in the first strike-related death, the murder of the (fictional) Italian immigrant, Carlo Michele, and thus marks the escalation of the conflict to a new, more desperate level. One character

6. Dale Fetherling, *Mother Jones: The Miners' Angel* (Carbondale, 1974), 85, 92, 103.

7. See *Investigation of Paint Creek Coal Fields of West Virginia,* 63d Cong., 2nd Sess., Senate Report No. 321. The Senate subcommittee responsible for the preparation of this report heard 2,291 pages of testimony (Fetherling, *Mother Jones,* 101).

recognizes what has happened: "They had killed a man, and nothing was ever going to be the same. She could hear the change like a creek swell, flooding nearer and nearer, and all the former things were passed away. It wouldn't never be the same, not in her lifetime, never the same, never the same, she kept saying over and over like a prayer, not knowing she was saying it out loud" (274). Michele, the scapegoat of the title, is used to satisfy some tacit need or desire by each side in the struggle. To the guards who kill him, he represents an opportunity to vent the frustrations generated by their frightening and morally questionable position; to the other Italians, he is a necessary offering, a relative newcomer sacrificed to satisfy the bloodthirst of the opposition; to the union leaders, he is a conveniently pathetic symbol of the mine owners' cruelty. Michele is himself a comparatively minor figure, baffled by "whispers on the wind [he] . . . couldn't understand" (110) and unable, to the moment of his death, to comprehend the forces by which he is being engulfed. As much as any character in the quintet, he demonstrates the ease with which an individual may become an object caught helplessly in the whirl of historical events.

Among the many perspectives from which Settle examines the scapegoating of Carlo Michele, a few gradually come to dominate, not because they appear most reliable (often they contradict one another), but because they are drawn from most extensively. "Headstrong, highhanded and highbrowed" Lily Lacey (6) is the daughter of a mine owner but a suffragette who sympathizes with the strikers; Jake Catlett is a friend and distant relation of the Laceys who nevertheless is among the leaders of the strike; Dan Neill, another relation, heads the detachment of hired guards; Neville Roundtree, an Englishman, manages a mine for its corporate owners; Eduardo Pagano is the ambitious young son of a Perugian mineworker. The drama played out among these figures and their friends and relations is, typically, characterized by mixed allegiances, hesitancies, and uncertain motives. In so inbred a community, in which constituencies are so economically and even emotionally interdependent, it seems nearly impossible for any person to participate in a violently divisive conflict without some ambivalence about that participation. Only the outsiders, in both camps, appear capable of acting without regret, since only they "[aren't] kin to anybody and . . . hadn't been raised with anybody" (54).

By far the most consequential of these outsiders is Mother Jones, the eighty-two-year-old union agitator, who, after Cromwell, plays the most extensive role of any actual historical figure in the quintet. Mother Jones, whose real name was Mary Harris Jones, spent much of 1912 and 1913 in West Virginia, encouraging the miners and harassing the mine owners and politicians, and Settle draws heavily on her documented language and habits in constructing a fictional facsimile. A number of her favorite expressions, such as referring to West Virginia's governor William E. Glasscock as "Crystal Peter" (199), find their way into *The Scapegoat,* where she becomes both a symbol of worker resistance and one of the many viewpoints through which events are apprehended.[8] Like Cromwell, Mother Jones is a historical figure distinctive enough to require little fictional embellishment. Also like Cromwell, she demonstrates how those committed to absolute positions, and thus to shifting consciously the currents of history, must choose to forgo the sorts of personal involvement that make absolutism impossible. Where Cromwell is a figure of tyrannical authority, Mother Jones is a populist, so in a sense they represent the extremes of the quintet's ideological spectrum. They embody "the right and the left in their entrenchments" (77), between whom most of the more ambivalent characters in the novels—characters distracted by commitments to family or tradition—attempt to exist. Both, however, are willing enough to manipulate the longings, fears, and even anguish of their followers to accomplish some ultimate purpose. Mother Jones's immediate response to the murder of Carlo Michele, an admonition to "use it" (275), is both heartless and impassioned and cannot help but remind even the sympathetic reader of Cromwell's desire to use Johnny Church and Thankful Perkins. Father Cromwell and Mother Jones are alike in their readiness to take advantage of their children's reverence.

The shift from paternal to maternal figures of authority is one indi-

8. "'You can expect no help from such a goddamned dirty coward,' [Mother Jones] reportedly told them, 'whom, for modesty's sake, we shall call "Crystal Peter." But I warn this little Governor that unless he rids Paint Creek and Cabin Creek of these goddamned Baldwin-Felts mine-guard thugs, there is going to be one hell of a lot of bloodletting in this hills'" (Fetherling, *Mother Jones,* 86–87). Settle notes: "Right at the end [of composing the novel], I found stenographic transcripts of three of [Mother Jones's] speeches. . . . They left me clues to Mother Jones's rhythm, her phrases" (Shattuck, "Talk with Settle," 43).

cation of what might be described as the gradual "feminization" of the quintet, a process that begins prior to, but becomes clearly evident in, *The Scapegoat*. The cultures in which the earlier novels are set dictate that the opportunities to perform heroic action and to challenge authority, at least publicly, be afforded almost exclusively to male characters. The area within which women operate in these cultures is too limited and private to allow for the overtly consequential gestures of a Johnny Church or a Jonathan Lacey. Resistance to authority is demonstrated through such customarily masculine activities as fighting (or refusing to fight) and entering a forbidden wilderness, whereas the women remain either absent (as in *Prisons*) or dependent on choices made by others (as in *O Beulah Land* and *Know Nothing*). But "as the physical frontiers shrink," notes Jane Gentry Vance, "the men tend to lose vision and strength until, in the last two novels, it is the women who realize in their characters the human potential for free and fruitful being."[9] This change results from no growing deficiency in the male character, just as the earlier passivity of the women results from no inherent deficiency in the female; rather, it indicates a slow alteration in the dimensions of heroic action. As authority becomes too pervasive to be challenged in combat and as the unexplored wilderness disappears, men trapped by traditional images of themselves as warriors and conquerors wither in frustration. At the same time, women accustomed to subtler, more internalized forms of resistance begin to play more prominent communal roles. The difference between Johnny and Jake Catlett, or between Sally and Lily Lacey, is partially one of historical and cultural context.

By and large, the men in *The Scapegoat* appear to themselves powerless and diminished, a self-perception they use sometimes as an excuse for indecision or inaction. Beverley Lacey laments his life but not, as the narrator makes clear, for what he himself has done: " 'I'm cold, just cold. Born in the middle. Born between things.' . . . Things had been done for him, a background prepared, the decisions all made, the worrying all taken care of by somebody else" (36). Dan Neill, "God's gift, Captain Dan from Beulah, their pride and joy, thoughtless, fast-moving, a fine horseman," is bitter with disappointment and frustra-

9. Vance, "History Inherited, History Created," 51.

tion, "stranded . . . in the only job a Neill could get after the Senator had brought so many to their knees along with him" (72). Jake Catlett, "strung between Beverley and the union, both of them pulling hard" (54), suffers a loss of judgment and motivation. Even percipient and reflective Neville Roundtree, who in another place and time might have been a Johnny Church, feels caught up in the pervasive impotence: "He saw a vast and senseless power that fed itself on its own body. He saw intelligence, this time a tiny bitter David, again with Lily's face. He saw himself and Jake Catlett and McLeod and the others, even Mr. Lacey who didn't do much, between the two forces, just trying to get the coal out and wanting to be left alone. That amorphous and pulsing power source was even interfering with his falling in love" (76). Earlier in the quintet, the male characters had acted out the role of a mythic female, Antigone; now, at least in the eyes of Roundtree, a female character is acting out the analogous role of an archetypal male, David, occupying the position of principled defiance. Like the women of earlier generations, the men of this generation use their subservience to a larger force as a justification for blindness and passivity. Settle has explained this attitude in one of her interviews: "In many Southern men, the inherited sense of responsibility to their families is too big for them. The loss of the Civil War did something to them, as if for 50 years, more even, they remained in a position of apology. . . . They lost the sense of escape."[10] Only men like Eduardo Pagano, for whom America in the twentieth century is still an unexplored mystery and whose Promised Land remains undiscovered, want more than "to be left alone."

The most forceful characters in the novel are female: joining Mother Jones, who seems a concentrated version of maternal will, are such women as Ann Lacey, Beverley's wife, and Annunziata Pagano, Eduardo's mother, both of whom dominate familial and communal life and make most of the story's difficult decisions. The narrator's description of Ann Lacey's bitter distinction between her husband and herself captures the difference between many of the novel's men and women: "He took everything for granted, and she believed in taking the bull by the horns. That was the difference between them and always had been" (29). Because the women have no history of independent decision

10. Shattuck, "Talk with Settle," 44.

making, the straitened circumstances of the present are far less frustrating for them than for the men; the decline in male vigor, in fact, seems to provide greater opportunity for female activity and autonomy. Especially for the young women, who in earlier novels were condemned to the dependency of a Melinda Lacey, the situation in 1912 is more energizing than debilitating. Freed by economic and social upheaval from their accustomed roles, they become more self-defining than any women in the quintet since Hannah Bridewell.

The nearest thing to a protagonist in *The Scapegoat* is Lily Lacey, the first female character in this long, multivolumed work to be faced with a genuine choice between freedom and obedience. Settle acknowledges Lily's place in the progression: "Johnny Church in *Prisons* is Jonathan Lacey in *O Beulah Land,* and becomes Johnny Catlett in *Know Nothing,* who fails. He becomes Lily in *The Scapegoat.*"[11] Unlike her male predecessors, however, Lily enters the novel late and plays a relatively peripheral role in its central action. Not until the start of Part II, ninety pages in, does the reader confront Lily directly, and thereafter hers remains only one among many interwoven stories. Earlier, she does seem to monopolize the consciousness of many characters in the novel: in Part I she is alluded to by nearly every internal voice, so that she appears to enter the narrative in tantalizing fragments, and at least two of the central male characters, Dan Neill and Neville Roundtree, are in love with her. Most of the others recognize that what Neill calls her "fool ideas" are uncharacteristic of the region and the age.

Lily's dilemma is another version of Johnny Church's original one: to remain safely within the comforting but suffocating circle of family and tradition or to act out of conscience and suffer isolation or worse. Educated at Vassar and conversant with the discourse of feminism and socialism, she wants desperately to assume her place among those effecting political and social change; at the same time, like nearly every character in the quintet, she feels bound to and sometimes seduced by the familiarity and easy acceptance of home. In contrast to Johnny Church, whose moment of decision rushes to meet him, Lily must seek one out, finding it eventually in the confrontation between the miners, with whom she is politically and morally sympathetic, and the group

11. *Ibid.,* 44.

of owners, which includes her father. Looking back on the conflict four years later, she recalls the climactic instant when she paused between the strikers' camp and home: "Shall I go down across the valley, or shall I go home? She heard that question as if she had spoken it aloud to the Ancre valley in front of her. She had known then, in a piercing moment when choice was alive in her whole body, that if she turned toward home, the choice would not come again, not until she was too old, and had sick headaches like her mother. I was like Antigone, standing there, she told herself" (168). For the first time since *Prisons,* the myth of Antigone and Creon is consciously invoked by a central character, and once again the protagonist chooses to side with Antigone. The comparison with the Greek heroine has been well prepared for, however, because all throughout *The Scapegoat* can be heard echoes of Johnny Church's thoughts about Antigone. The image to which Church keeps returning in his dilemma is that of Antigone turning her wrist and shaking the foundations of the state. Here, by comparison, is Dan Neill's vision of the frustrating Lily: "Her wrist turned as it had, separate and alive, on the porch where she stood in the shadows, as if at last she'd made up her mind about something, and she grasped the rope of the hammock, pulling it away, rejecting it, and turned and walked off the porch around the house without even thinking to say goodbye" (70).

Despite her evocation of Antigone, Lily's decision is not nearly as politically consequential as Johnny Church's. Neither the strikers, who believe her to be acting "out of curiosity and boredom" (199), nor her parents take seriously her radical gesture of separation. But her choice is nonetheless the beginning of a movement away from home that carries her eventually to New York City, then to voluntary service and death in World War I. Although it is exacted less quickly and dramatically, the price she pays for freedom is in the end as high as the price paid by Johnny Church. And since the reader learns of Lily's death, in a flash forward, before her moment of decision arrives, the path she selects can be recognized at once as costly.

Lily also serves as the bridge between West Virginia in 1912 and the temporally and geographically distanced cataclysm of World War I. One of the novel's longest flash forwards carries her from the Kanawha River to the river Ancre in France, where, in 1916, she is serving as a nurse in a volunteer aid detachment. Although the war figures less prominently in *The Scapegoat* than do the English revolution, the American Revolution, or the Civil War in the previous novels, the brief shift to 1916 is a reminder that world conflict looms menacingly over the events of 1912, undermining plans and dwarfing, by contrast, the violence paralyzing the mining town. The reader's knowledge of the war-caused deaths of Lily and Neville Roundtree casts an aura of ironic futility over the characters' actions in the novel's present; Lily's description of "over a hundred and fifty men . . . killed by one machine gun" near the Somme (170) renders ominous the Gatling gun perched, in 1912, on the Laceys' porch. Glimpses of wholesale slaughter trivialize yet at the same time invest with greater value the communal anguish over a single needless death. Generally the juxtaposition of the present strike and the coming war places the action into a historical context that suggests, again, the near impossibility of controlling or even reliably predicting the direction of events. In a novel where virtually every character looks anxiously toward the future, none can anticipate the future that actually awaits.

Because of its shifting time frame and because of the tendency of its characters to glance continually backward and forward, *The Scapegoat* highlights the situation of the present as a moment suspended between a past and a future. Its individuals bring to current circumstances memories of a history and well- or ill-defined hopes of an existence to come—memories and hopes that shape their behavior and evolve as circumstances change. Recollection of the past and anticipation of the future, ordinarily understood as dramatically different or even oppositional processes, are here understood as fundamentally similar. Both are "censored by self-comforting" and insulated by a "protective covering" (175), that is, subject to the pressure of the identical fears and desires. The belief that because events in the past have already happened they are more fixed, less subject to variations in perception, than events in the future is, as I have been arguing, undermined by the form and content of the novel. "Nostalgia," Lily recognizes, "consists of remembering things that never were that way" (160), just as hoping consists of imagining things that have not yet been: in neither case is there necessarily a connection between events as defined by the individual and some verifiable, commonly agreed upon reality. Two related terms, lying and dreaming, are used insistently in *The Scapegoat* to describe this personal fashioning of the future and past.

From the beginning, the quintet has struggled to distinguish between what it means to lie, to reshape the past or present in the service of some personal need, and to dream, to imagine the future, and perhaps the present and past as well, in the service of that same need. Is Cromwell lying or dreaming when he claims to be executing Johnny Church for the good of the nation? Is Sally Lacey lying or dreaming when she superimposes tidewater culture on tramontane Virginia? Is Johnny Catlett lying or dreaming when he defends a South he knows is doomed and mistaken? Questions like these, raised tangentially in the earlier novels, are central to *The Scapegoat,* where the difficulty of distinguishing between lying and dreaming serves as a virtual refrain. "Recall," or memory, "was like a dream, too, the same fragments, some etched, pure vision, then spaces, then other vivid scenes" (158). That lies can be destructive is clear enough in a novel devoted to "watching a lie begin, one of those lies where nothing was said but you acted like something happened you really knew didn't" (84); but that lies can be protective and therapeutic, can "cover the stone poverty of . . . real memory" (237), is clear as well. Dreams, too, can be "safe and abiding" (110–11), like Carlo Michele's, or destructive as "a thread that seemed as soft as silk until you drew it through your fingers to sew with it and it cut like a razor" (236). The point here is not only that lies may be less avoidable than one imagines and dreams less comforting but that the urge to reconstruct and evade reality is powerful and assumes a variety of forms.

Implicit in this assertion of the virtual universality of lying and dreaming is a question that haunts the entire quintet and is addressed most directly at the conclusion of *The Scapegoat*. That is, is it possible to distinguish between constructive and destructive ways of subjectively refashioning reality? Are certain, identifiable kinds of lying and dreaming sustaining, whereas others are ennervating or corrosive? Lily's final act is to confront this dilemma as she rides the train away from home and toward New York City and self-reliance:

> Lily looked back at Montaigne, trying to see the words, but her eyes bleared with tears. She couldn't understand why she always boohooed like that when she left home after all her hoping and dreaming. She blinked the

> tears away so she could see the page. "A brilliant and sharp clarity is needed to kill people; our life is too real and substantial for supernatural fantastical incidents." It was like Essie dipping into the Bible. It was telling her to stop sitting there sunk in hopes and tears when she still had a job to do. (277)

The point here seems to be that one should embrace the "real and substantial" and avoid as far as possible unproductive "hoping and dreaming." Yet moments later, in the novel's final paragraph, Lily (along, I think, with Settle) qualifies this advice: "She didn't know where [Eduardo] was going when he got off at Covington, but she knew at last where she was going. She leaned back and dreamed and didn't care what Montaigne said. There was clarity in dreams, too. She dreamed, lulled by the train, of getting off at heaven or New York City, whichever she got to first" (278).

From the story of Lily, and from its earlier enactments by the various Johnny characters, emerges at least a tentative definition of positive and negative dreaming. Those dreams that lead to action, self-definition, and the transcendence of circumstances, such as Lily's or Jonathan Lacey's, possess what Lily calls "clarity"; those that lead to paralysis, erasure of the self, and mere fantasizing, such as Althea's or Sally Lacey's, lack both clarity and utility. Characters in this world may be divided not into those who do and do not dream but into those whose dreams are and are not original and inspirational. Hannah McKarkle makes a similar distinction, I think, in the last novel of the quintet, *The Killing Ground:* "It has not been Johnny's death that has evaded me, it has been more; it was what was done with his death by all of us, not the event, but the release or the self-imprisonment afterwards; the substitutions, as if he were an object of desire and not a separate man" (339). The difference between desire as release and desire as self-imprisonment is comparable to the difference I am noting here between that dreaming which is creative and that which is destructive. Many of the quintet's central characters dream creatively and are in this sense artists who imaginatively arrange the material of their worlds into meaningful, coherent fictions. The work of the novelist becomes one example—perhaps the definitive example—of a creative act that may assume a wide variety of forms.

*The Scapegoat* is the novel that tests most relentlessly the stylistic and structural limits of Settle's technique. Her desire to re-create the spoken language of the past blossoms here into a chorus of individualized West Virginia voices, and her tendency to empathize with all sides in any historical conflict generates a multiplicity of contradictory viewpoints. To a greater extent than in any of her other novels, the traditional bases of narrative fiction are abandoned: plot is no more important here than in *Mrs. Dalloway* or *Ulysses,* and even the novel's central characters are, by ordinary standards, obliquely glimpsed. Suspense and sympathetic identification—in the sense that we identify with Johnny Church and worry about his eventual fate—are sacrificed in the interests of immediacy and historical objectivity. If *Prisons* is the most intimate and moving of Settle's books and, by her own admission, the most self-revelatory, *The Scapegoat* is the most technically self-conscious and openly experimental. Written only five years apart, they represent opposite poles between which all Settle's other fiction may be situated.

In one important respect, *The Scapegoat* is peculiarly representative of Settle's career: as she has been difficult to classify as a novelist, so this novel has been unusually difficult to categorize and contextualize. From the start I have been considering the Beulah quintet in relation to a number of traditions and genres, defining the sequence as a hybrid of European and American tendencies and contrasting *O Beulah Land* and *Know Nothing* with conventional tales of the frontier and the antebellum South. It is nearly impossible to talk about *The Scapegoat* in these terms. Its temporal and geographic setting has generated no distinct tradition of historical re-creation, fictional or otherwise, and thus the novel cannot be seen, like a number of its predecessors, as violating expectations or demythologizing a glorified past.[12] Set in the early part of this century, it skirts the scarcely discernible line between historical and contemporary fiction. The story is both heavily dependent on documentary evidence, in the manner of the traditional historical novel, and told in a style that recalls the modernist and postmodernist works that reject traditional forms of narrative. *The Scapegoat* even manages to blend the reportorial precision that marks the historical fiction of Capote or Mailer with the reflexivity and mythological resonance of works by Fowles or Barth. The novel seems less a combination than an avoidance of expected genres and categories.

12. A number of novels have been written about the northern Missouri and West Virginia mine wars, including Jack Conroy's *The Disinherited* (1933) and, much more recently, Denise Giardina's *Storming Heaven* (1987).

The emphasis in *The Scapegoat* on class conflict and management-labor relationships would seem to suggest a connection to the union or proletarian novels popular, or at least widely written, during the nineteen-thirties especially. One needs to look to novels like Robert Cantwell's *The Land of Plenty* and William Rollins' *The Shadow Before,* both published in 1934, to find representations of the early union movements and portraits of union leaders comparable in exhaustiveness to Settle's. In style and polemical intent, however, this fiction bears little resemblance to *The Scapegoat*. The radical novel, according to Walter Rideout, is designed to attack a particular socioeconomic system and explicitly "advocates that the system be fundamentally changed." Although *The Scapegoat,* characteristically, sides implicitly with Antigone in its version of the Creon-Antigone conflict, the strategy of narrative objectivity disqualifies the novel as a work of radical social criticism. Because of their determination to create socially and politically efficacious art, moreover, radical novelists favor what Michael Gold, in a major theoretical statement, defines as "proletarian realism": such fiction requires "technical precision in the description of proletarian employment," sentences of "as few words as possible," and plots comprised of "swift action, clear form, the direct line, cinema in words," in short, accessible, meticulously realistic pictures of working-class life. The accessibility of the form is meant, in part, to enhance its political effectiveness. By these standards, *The Scapegoat* is neither swift, direct, nor accessible, and it shares the bourgeois emphasis on aesthetic value that the proletarian realists emphatically rejected.[13] Settle's union novel, in sum, bears only the vaguest resemblance to conventional union fiction.

One way of accounting for the strangeness of *The Scapegoat* is by clarifying its role in the quintet. The last of the novels to be conceived, it acts as a bridge between the chronicles of Beulah detailed in *O Beulah Land* and *Know Nothing,* and the contemporary social analysis of *The Killing Ground:* the older age is visible only in fragments, the newer, only in stirrings and omens. And though those two ages are relatively familiar to most readers, one from artistic re-creations, the other from personal experience, the moment of intersection seems alien and inchoate. If historical fiction normally engages a reader's expectations

13. Walter Rideout, *The Radical Novel in the United States, 1900–1954* (Cambridge, Mass., 1956), 12; Michael Gold, "Proletarian Realism," *New Masses,* VI (1930), 5.

about the represented period, *The Scapegoat* is an abnormal historical novel in having so few expectations to engage. Settle, however, views the book as an essential addition to the sequence. "How can you write about coal country without writing about the mine wars? . . . One of the reasons for the failure of *Fight Night on a Sweet Saturday* was that I didn't know enough about [the protagonists'] parents. So it became kind of pathetic" (Appendix B, p. 162). *The Scapegoat* not only dramatizes the consequences of Johnny Catlett's loss of will in *Know Nothing* but provides the basis for the frustrations and conflicts of ensuing generations. "The resonances from Althea, from Jake Catlett's daddy, from all of them in *The Scapegoat,* give the later characters a reason for being and give you an understanding you didn't have before" (Appendix B, p. 162). Before that understanding could become complete, however, the failed *Fight Night* had to be transformed into *The Killing Ground* and the lessons of the past brought to bear on a mystifying present.

# *The Killing Ground* Dark Nostalgia 6

In many of the best-known spiritual autobiographies, the path transcribed is circular: like William Wordsworth revisiting the banks of the Wye or Pip wandering again through the garden of Miss Havisham's house, the protagonist, wiser and more temperate, returns after a journey of suffering and redemption to the point of the journey's beginning. T. S. Eliot, in his own self-exploration, defines not only the movement of the *Four Quartets* but a broad religious and literary tradition when he writes that "the end of all our exploring / Will be to arrive where we started / And know the place for the first time."[1] It should not surprise, therefore, that *The Killing Ground* marks the conclusion of a "perilous wandering, perilous meaning circular" (6); that the novel's setting, the fictional city of Canona, West Virginia, is situated on the ruins of an ancient "sacred circle" (11); or that the plot traces an elaborate, slowly unfolding "circle of time and circumstance" (365). Its protagonist, Hannah McKarkle, explores both "the confined circle of [her] own life" (8) and the more "spacious circle" (6) of familial and regional development. This last novel encompasses the starting and ending points of the quintet, clarifying both the origins and the fruits of Settle's long exercise in historical reconstruction. "All the digging, all the questioning, all the past I'd harrowed" ends after a quarter-

1. T. S. Eliot, *The Complete Poems and Plays* (New York, 1971), 145.

century, for McKarkle and for her creator, "in that valley where it had begun" (376). *The Killing Ground* dramatizes the personal source of the conflicts and themes that animate five novels and, in the end, reveals the power of those novels to lay to rest the most troubling of personal demons. Rarely has any work or series of works so self-consciously turned back on itself to explore its own meaning and importance.

Even the publication history of *The Killing Ground* is peculiarly circular, with Settle revisiting the story of Hannah and Johnny McKarkle after nearly twenty years and, to paraphrase Eliot, knowing it for the first time. In 1964 she had published *Fight Night on a Sweet Saturday* to complete the trilogy begun with *O Beulah Land* and *Know Nothing,* carrying to 1960 the interwoven family histories related in the earlier novels. This concluding novel was, in Settle's own view, "a failure" not just because it received "very, very bad reviews" (Appendix B, p. 161) but because the chronological leap, from Johnny Catlett setting off to fight the Civil War in 1861 to Johnny McKarkle dying in a drunk tank in 1960, was too abrupt and the treatment of the later characters, Settle's contemporaries, too unsympathetic. It suffered, moreover, from some ill-advised editing. The novel originally included a section set in 1907 (shortly before the time of *The Scapegoat*) that described Hannah's mother as a girl and provided at least a small bridge between the nineteenth-century and contemporary episodes. However, at the insistence of editors who wanted "to sell the book as a 'modern' novel," the section was removed and the process of trying to empathize with Sally Brandon Neill made more difficult.[2] The problem of too abrupt a leap she solved with the publication of *The Scapegoat;* the problem of too little sympathy demanded the dramatic revision of *Fight Night,* but only after the passage of time had matured Settle as a novelist and placed the events of the early 1960s into a broader historical context. *Fight Night on a Sweet Saturday* is a novel of contemporary life; *The Killing Ground* is a historical novel, not only because the occurrences in 1960 are juxtaposed with others in 1978 and 1980, but because, like the historical novels identified by Avrom Fleishman, it is marked by "the active presence of a concept of history as a shaping force."[3] It acts as a fitting

2. Mary Lee Settle, "The Search for Beulah Land," *Southern Review,* n.s., XXIV (1988), 24. See also Appendix B, p. 000.

3. Fleishman, *English Historical Novel,* 15.

conclusion to the quintet in part because its underlying subject is the meaning of living in and writing about history.

The long opening section of the novel, set in June, 1978, describes the return of novelist Hannah McKarkle to her hometown of Canona after a protracted period of semivoluntary exile. Ostensibly she returns as a "famous personality" (29) to speak at an art gallery fund-raiser. Actually she is drawn again to investigate the event that has haunted her life and art for the past two decades: the pathetic death of her older brother Johnny, victim of a drunken jailhouse brawl in 1960. "I want to know who killed my brother," she reminds herself. "Oh, we all know a name, but beyond the hand that did it, I want to know why and I still intend to find out" (134). Events in 1978 evoke and blend together with memories of Hannah's history; the abrupt suicide of Charley Bland, reminiscent of the death of Johnny, leads to the ritualistic reenactment of the mourning of 1960 and the intensification of Hannah's "dark nostalgia" (46). Dominating both the story's present and the recollected past is Hannah's sense of estrangement from a family unwilling to understand her chosen role and from friends goaded by her rejection of their ceremonies and values.

This précis barely hints at the demands of what may be the most complex portion of any novel in the quintet. To begin with, summarizing the events of Part I as if they formed a straightforward, chronologically ordered plot is misleading. Whether one considers the action "a series of circlings around events" or, less charitably, a "meander[ing] through numerous past and present scenes," the indirection and ambiguity of the long opening section are daunting.[4] To some degree the narrative strategy of *The Scapegoat* is here continued: the represented world is, at least at the start, an amalgam of various points of view, each characterized by biases, misjudgments, and habits of discourse distinct from the others. Unlike *The Scapegoat,* however, *The Killing Ground* includes a first-person voice that first competes with, then finally overwhelms, the less fully developed third-person voices. Hannah McKarkle's first-person perspective alternates in Part I with a third-person perspective that is filtered through the minds of nearly a dozen different

4. Garrett, *Understanding Mary Lee Settle,* 75; Bruce Allen, Review of *The Killing Ground,* in *Christian Science Monitor,* August 13, 1982, p. B-3.

characters, generating, even more often than the *The Scapegoat,* multiple, conflicting versions of the same moment or scene. Chronological leaps occur frequently and suddenly, particularly within the narrative of Hannah, whose memory is active and liable to be triggered by nearly anything she sees or hears:

> Two hours later I reached the high savannah of Greenbriar, and turned south on the country road. I had to slow down. The road was narrow, but that was not the only reason. I was almost to Fairy Land Cave, where the first Hannah had climbed, all day long, up the face of the cliff. I had hiked in a long line of Girl Scouts, along a concrete walk into the cave mouth. There was a line of naked electric lights along the path. Everything had names. . . . The cave was clammy inside. There was nothing left to fear. But when the guide turned off the line of electric lights, it had been, for a minute, ancient and blind, a black pressure against my eyes, as heavy as death, as it had been the first time I had entered it, a wild black tunnel. My brother Johnny told me it was Dead Man's Cave. A man had been lost in it and starved to death. I was seven years old. (125–26)

This paragraph is typically difficult, moving among at least four different points in time with few markers to signal the shifts. The opening lines take place in the novel's present, 1978, until the reference to "the first Hannah" carries the reader back to Hannah Bridewell in the eighteenth century. The next sentence ("I had hiked") moves to Hannah McKarkle's childhood, where the paragraph remains until the movement even deeper into the past in "as it had been the first time." The legend of the starved man, of course, superimposes yet another image on a scene already crowded with memories that are both simultaneous and spread across time. Only three paragraphs later does the narrative return, briefly and with little warning, to the novel's present.

Settle is here carrying to an extreme a strategy employed by many writers of circular autobiography. When Wordsworth returns to Tintern Abbey, he sees not merely the landscape in 1798 but images of himself in 1793 and the 1780s; when Pip explores the empty ruins of Miss Havisham's house, he can "trace out," in his mind, "where every part of the old house had been, and where the brewery had been, and where the gates, and where the casks."[5] In these older works, however, the essential separation between present and past, between witnessed

5. Charles Dickens, *Great Expectations* (1860; rpr. New York, 1965), 491.

and recollected events, is preserved by the ordinary devices of language: verb tense, syntax, sentence and paragraph structure, and so on. In *The Killing Ground* these ordering devices are less helpful (in the paragraph above, for instance, both the past and past perfect tenses refer to more than one time frame), and the fusion of present and past is more absolute. Experience and remembrance become virtually simultaneous acts.

Although *The Killing Ground* may not be, as Nancy Carol Joyner suggests, "impossible to appreciate without having read the entire series," it is likely to confuse readers unacquainted with the many fictional names and places to which it insistently alludes. Even those familiar with the previous novels may have to struggle, especially at the start, to make sense of the connections between this concluding volume and its predecessors. Hannah McKarkle seems the child of the entire quintet: daughter of *The Scapegoat*'s Mooney McKarkle and Sally Brandon Neill, granddaughter of *Know Nothing*'s Lacey Kregg, great-granddaughter of Johnny Catlett and Melinda Lacey, and so on, back to Johnny Church and Gideon MacKarkle of *Prisons*. At least a dozen other characters in *The Killing Ground* are descended in a dizzying variety of ways from characters in the earlier books. Several central figures in *The Scapegoat,* including Althea Lacey, Jake Catlett, Eddie Pagano, and Mooney McKarkle, reappear now a half-century later and in some cases are scarcely recognizable. Most important, Hannah McKarkle is the first character in the quintet whose knowledge of her familial and regional history is comparable to the reader's—the first "who realizes implicitly," according to Peggy Bach, "her own personal past"—and therefore the first to refer frequently (and reliably) to names, places, and events in the previous novels.[6] Comparisons that might have been implied in *Know Nothing* or *The Scapegoat* are here made directly and self-consciously.

Not all the connections between *The Killing Ground* and the earlier volumes are explicit and familial; some are allusive and structural. From its opening paragraphs, the novel recapitulates the important images, tropes, and themes of the quintet:

> It is five o'clock in the morning. Daylight Saving Time. I have been sitting on the balcony of the downriver room on the second floor of the

6. Joyner, "Mary Lee Settle's Connections," 44; Bach, "Searching Voice," 846.

> Howard Johnson's motel on Canona Boulevard almost all night. In other cities motels may be escape routes to anonymity, but not for me, not in Canona, and not this morning.
>
> In the first twilight of dawn, the Canona River moves like a silver snake under a suspension of white mist. The still-unlit south hills, under the lush cover of trees, are primordial across the river. The hollow where my ancestor and namesake Hannah woke over two hundred years ago is a dark gash between them. But the tree she crawled in to sleep, on its mound of earth, is gone, covered by the retaining wall of the road to the suburbs. (3)

Hannah McKarkle reminiscing silently in the Howard Johnson's on Canona Boulevard recalls Johnny Church on the road to Burford; the Canona River moving "like a silver snake" re-creates the "great flat valley of the Thames" (*Prisons,* 15); the "suspension of white mist" echoes the "fog . . . so dense" of the English morning (*Prisons,* 26). As Hannah herself recognizes, moreover, the landscape described here is precisely the one described at the start of *O Beulah Land,* "where my ancestor and namesake Hannah woke over two hundred years ago." *Know Nothing* also begins with a river and the thrashing struggle of Johnny Catlett to swim. In each case, the setting embodies a tension between permanence and change, the primordial hills and the vanished tree, as well as the flow of great and small events by which the individual in history is carried along. The "strong river of time and circumstance" (89), that is, runs from the quintet's opening page. Other literal and figurative images, prisons, roots, rings, riding crops, are similarly recurrent, and even the titles of earlier novels are slyly embedded in this final text: the "O Beulah Land" hymn is heard on a car radio (227), Hannah is schooled to be a "know-nothing girl" (155), and Johnny is "made the scapegoat" (190) for the indiscretions of others.

*The Killing Ground* is also the point of intersection between the quintet and Settle's fiction of contemporary southern life. The reappearance of characters from *The Love Eaters* and *The Clam Shell* means that familiarity with what George Garrett calls the "other novels from Beulah land" is nearly as important as familiarity with *The Scapegoat* or *Know Nothing.*[7] *The Clam Shell* in particular, because it includes many of *The Killing Ground*'s supporting players, may be considered part of the foundation of the later novel and very nearly as a sixth chapter in

7. Garrett, *Understanding Mary Lee Settle,* 82.

the extended sequence. Set mostly in 1936, it fills in some of the empty space between *The Scapegoat* and *The Killing Ground* and anatomizes West Virginia manners and values comparably to the way the novels in the quintet do. Its narrator-protagonist is neither Hannah McKarkle nor Mary Lee Settle but a woman at odds with family and culture who bears a strong resemblance to both. Certainly her autobiographical narrative clarifies the forces and institutions by which a person like Hannah McKarkle would have been formed.

*Charley Bland* sheds additional light on Hannah, though from a different perspective. Published seven years after *The Killing Ground,* it revisits some of the same literal and thematic territory and explores with the same intensity both the corrosive effects of familial pressures and the shapes, frightening or beautiful, assumed by love, but the focus in this case is more exclusively on failed romance. Once again the narrator-protagonist resembles but is not Hannah McKarkle or Mary Lee Settle, and once again characters from *The Love Eaters, The Clam Shell,* and *The Killing Ground* play familiar, if slightly revised, roles. Although a case might be made for including both *The Clam Shell* and *Charley Bland* among the Beulah novels, on balance they appear more peripherally than organically related to the other five. Settle has called *The Clam Shell* "the closest thing to an autobiographical novel [she] ever wrote" and might say the same of *Charley Bland.* As a result, the action in neither is wholly compatible with the less autobiographical action in the quintet. Details and chronology are not always consistent with those in *The Killing Ground,* and though some of the themes of the quintet figure in *The Clam Shell* and *Charley Bland,* they tend to be less prominent and to be conveyed through a different set of images and myths. Ultimately, in relation to the quintet, *Charley Bland* may be considered a coda or, better, an exorcism, for it seems Settle's attempt to rid herself finally of the haunting obsessions of four decades. "Maybe with the end of this story," the narrator hopes, "the unknown people will no longer be haunted and can forget at last that we ever existed."[8]

Woven into the fictional tapestry of *The Killing Ground* is yet another thread of complexity. Hannah McKarkle is not merely a novelist. Her

8. Garrett, *Understanding Mary Lee Settle,* 91; Mary Lee Settle, *Charley Bland* (New York, 1989), 206.

introducer at the art gallery fund-raiser notes: "She is the author of numerous works of fiction including *Prison* I mean *Prisons O Beulah Land Know Nothing*. She is working on a novel about the coal business in 1912 called *The Scapegoat*" (39). Thus this protagonist and sometime narrator is supposedly the creator of the novels to which *The Killing Ground* is the sequel. The purpose of this unusual though not unique fictional strategy is fairly clear. Only a character thoroughly familiar with events in the previous novels—only, in other words, their author or reader—could make "simply and directly" the necessary connections between those events and the action of *The Killing Ground*, and calling Hannah the creator of those novels is surely less awkward than calling her the reader.[9] The ambiguities thereby introduced, nonetheless, are staggering. Since Hannah is the author of the Beulah novels, is it fair to assume that her thoughts and judgments are identical to Mary Lee Settle's? Since characters from Hannah's novels appear and are alluded to by other characters in *The Killing Ground*, should one assume that those earlier fictions are factual? What are the implications, that is, of Eddie Pagano's being both a character in Hannah McKarkle's *The Scapegoat* and an acquaintance of Hannah McKarkle in *The Killing Ground?* This Hannah calls Hannah Bridewell her "namesake" (3), but is she named after some actual Hannah or has she named a purely fictional Hannah after herself? As thoroughly as in the most self-reflexive experimental fiction, the borders between the worlds inside and outside the language of the text are obscured.

One thing, at least, is clear from Settle's comments about *The Killing Ground:* Hannah McKarkle is a fictional construct who should no more be identified with the author than should Edouard of *Les Faux-Monnayeurs,* creator of a novel called *Les Faux-Monnayeurs,* be identified with André Gide. To begin with, there are a number of straightforward biographical differences between the author and her creation, as Settle herself has noted. "She is of a younger generation, an Eisenhower child. My own youth was in another time and another world. . . . My brother is alive, my father was not a lawyer and coal owner, but a civil engineer." And though one need not accept at face value Settle's claim that "little of the new Hannah is myself," there are signs in the novel of her desire

9. Garrett, *Understanding Mary Lee Settle,* 79.

to distinguish between author and character.[10] The shifts between first and third person provide the reader with a broader perspective than Hannah has and reveal implications and shades of character of which she is not wholly aware. Her responses and judgments, especially in the 1960 episodes but to an extent in the later ones as well, tend toward the impetuous and naïve. Like any reasonably reliable narrator, including Johnny Church, Hannah often voices what appears to be the author's sentiments, but she falls short of being the authoritative spokeswoman for the fiction of which she is a part.

In the opinion of some critics and reviewers, *The Killing Ground* collapses under the weight of this structural and stylistic complexity. For Jane Gentry Vance it is "in some respects the weakest of the five books"; for Joyner, who finds much to admire, it is "unfortunately self-conscious and redundant." Gail Godwin laments that "every time we begin to be eased into the stream of fiction, the voice of Hannah pulls us back with an interpretation of the events we are witnessing, the characters we are getting to know."[11] As Godwin's criticism suggests, complaints about the novel have come mostly from those who (reasonably enough) value the momentum of an orderly plot and the identification with fully developed characters. By comparison with its predecessors, *The Killing Ground* provides little of either. The plot is fragmentary, and with the exception of Hannah, the characters are briefly if vividly sketched. As the concluding novel in the quintet, it is inevitably forced to do the most complicated work, dramatizing its own story while tying together strands remaining from twelve hundred previous pages and, perhaps, sacrificing some customary narrative energy in the effort to synthesize and unify. The decision to make Hannah the author of the Beulah novels both allows this final chapter in Settle's American history to serve as a distillation of all the previous ones and creates an unusually self-referential and demanding text.

The demands ease considerably in Part II, where the story is carried back to 1960 and the events surrounding the death of Johnny McKarkle are recounted. The section is narrated entirely by Hannah, who for the most part arranges episodes in chronological order and speaks

10. Settle, "Search for Beulah Land," 25.

11. Vance, "History Inherited, History Created," 47; Joyner, "Mary Lee Settle's Connections," 44; Godwin, Review of *The Killing Ground,* 30.

here in a style less allusive and syntactically challenging than in Part I. One is presented, that is, with a relatively conventional, accessible fictional autobiography. While living in New York City, Hannah receives a drunken, late-night phone call from Johnny, who speaks, not for the first time apparently, the "magic words": "Come on down, Sissy, I need you" (165). She returns, as she always has, only to discover on arrival that Johnny, arrested for public intoxication, has been knocked down and critically injured while in jail. Her initial challenge is to wrestle with her own shock and the grief, often self-indulgent, of her family and friends; her subsequent and deeper challenge is to discover the direct and indirect causes of her brother's death. Clearly the most imposing among the obstacles she must overcome is her mother. "Dressed in tragedy and black linen" (253), determined that Hannah play the role of obedient daughter, Sally Brandon Neill McKarkle is in many ways the most compelling character in the novel and among the most frightening in the quintet. Hannah persists, however, and eventually learns that Johnny's killer was Jake Catlett, indigent son of Jake Catlett of *The Scapegoat* and distant relation of the Neills. The murder of Johnny McKarkle was, in effect, fratricide.

Because Part II of *The Killing Ground* includes most of the material carried over from *Fight Night on a Sweet Saturday,* its relative accessibility is unsurprising: in style and date of composition, much of the section is closer to *Know Nothing* than to *The Scapegoat*. The differences between the earlier and later versions, however, are substantial and revealing. Speaking from the vantage point of 1980, Hannah is considerably more self-critical than she had been in 1964; the cynicism of *Fight Night* (troublesome to several reviewers) has modulated into apologetic self-awareness. Her memories of that time, for example, are presented with a judgment already built in: "We drank a lot for art's sake, and were prepared to follow Jack Kerouac all the way to the suburbs. I thought all this was individual at the time. Now I see we were a crop fertilized with money" (155). A recollection of the West Virginia primary campaign of John F. Kennedy, nostalgic and disillusioned at once, solidifies the differences between the worlds Hannah inhabited then and now. In general, the 1960 incarnations of Hannah McKarkle and Canona are historicized as they could not have been in 1964 and, as fully as Johnny Church and England in 1649, are understood as products of a set of peculiar cultural circumstances. Together with the evolution of Settle's style between 1964 and 1980, this new perspective results in a substantially revised presentation of events, shown in a corresponding paragraph from each work:

> So when the telephone rang in my apartment in New York on the Saturday night before Labor Day in 1960, I didn't want to answer it. I was in bed with somebody. Now, I am ashamed to tell this, not because I was in love, or felt ecstatic or savage and wanted to protect myself from prying, or even sinful or afraid of getting caught. No, it was worse than that. It didn't really matter. That's how Johnny and I were, three years ago. It just didn't make a damn bit of difference, and I was proud that it didn't. Johnny and I were far too bright for that.[12]

> When the telephone rang in my bedroom in New York at one o'clock in the morning on the Saturday night before Labor Day, I knew at once who it was. I didn't want to answer it. Carlo Tarmino. I haven't thought of him in years, and I have trouble remembering what he looked like. Oh, yes, I see him, as that night with the light of 65th Street across his sleeping face, and then, his eyes flying open. Carlo was from Brooklyn, and beat as he was, a one o'clock phone call still triggered disaster. Carlo had moved in with me during the summer, and had turned the end of my living room into a studio. His paintings were abstract and very large. As soon as Carlo was awake, he, too, seemed to know who it was. (*Killing Ground,* 165–66)

The later version emphasizes the passage of time ("I haven't thought of him in years") and replaces Hannah's remarks about herself, a looking inward, with the precise, compressed description of Carlo Tarmino. That both she and Carlo "knew at once who it was" suggests the habitual nature of Johnny's intrusive phone calls and better explains Hannah's reluctance to answer this one. Whereas the movement from sentence to sentence is in the earlier version wholly coherent, the later includes an abrupt shift characteristic of Settle's mature style: "I didn't want to answer it. Carlo Tarmino." The specificity increases, too, from "my apartment in New York on the Saturday night before Labor Day" to "my bedroom in New York at one o'clock in the morning on the Saturday night before Labor Day," despite the change from recent to distant recollection.

In both versions of the story, the pivotal incident is the killing of

12. Mary Lee Settle, *Fight Night on a Sweet Saturday* (New York, 1964), 3.

Johnny McKarkle, or, more elementally, "the fury of one unknown fist hitting an unknown face" (153). Although this image appears only in the fifth novel, Settle identifies it as both the impetus for all five and the explosion to which the entire long narrative has been building. She explains the impelling force of the scene that came to her in 1954:

> I had, as a visual image, a scene—the detonator of a new book. I saw one man hit another, a stranger, in a jail's drunk tank on a hot Saturday night. When I began to seek out why, I realized that the gesture, the American explosion of violence in the single act, carried with it abandoned hopes, old hates and a residue of prejudices. To trace them, I knew that I was going to have to travel back to when the hates were new, the hopes alive, the prejudices merely contemporary fears.[13]

The quintet, that is, began with an image of sudden violence, the roots of which lay buried in American history and culture. Many of the central themes in the novels, including the tension between freedom and obedience, the interchangeability of oppressor and oppressed, and the contrast between reality and dream, become, finally, means of explaining this almost instinctive act of frustration and anger. Two cousins, one privileged, one lost, come together in the holding cell of a West Virginia jail. All the forces of history, family, and chance—mostly chance—that have pushed one into aimless ease have pushed the other into desperate poverty, erasing in the process all signs of the blood ties by which they are irrevocably joined. The destruction of one descendant of martyred Johnny Church by another is not, Settle insists, merely accidental but the nearly inevitable consequence of the conflicts and inequalities that typify American history. Church's refusal to submit, the changing social and economic positions of the Catletts and Laceys, the division between Johnny Catlett and his brother Lewis, the broken dreams of Dan Neill, all are encapsulated, somewhat pathetically, in the fatal confrontation between the two failed men.

Among the ways Settle unifies the quintet, no other is more effective than the repetition from novel to novel of a number of clearly defined character types, each of which embodies a recognizably American impulse or attitude. *The Killing Ground,* in the end, appears to classify those types with almost taxonomical precision. Jake Catlett is the final

13. Settle, "Recapturing the Past," 36.

incarnation of all the "impotent . . . rebels, the wild boys" (340), that is, the characters who reject so utterly the harness of authority and responsibility as to become isolated and destructive. Caught in the struggle between freedom and obedience, such characters, "poor anarchic Thompson, Doggo Cutwright, Peregrine Lacey, Indian killer, Big Dan O'Neill" (340), succumb not to mindless subservience, the most common failure, but to reckless independence and end by destroying others along with themselves. Johnny McKarkle, despite his name, does not reenact the crises of Johnny Church, Jonathan Lacey, and Johnny Catlett, or if he does, he does so at some point prior to the start of the novel. By the time he enters *The Killing Ground,* he has conceded defeat by allowing his family to "pull his heart and hamstrings until he was small enough to live with [them]" (343). The inverse of Jake Catlett, he has, like so many before him in the quintet, fallen victim to "the seduction of duty and comfort and compliance" (340) and been condemned to a life of ease without purpose or value. "Without land to till or people to care for," Hannah decides, "Johnny had been caught in a parody where the land had shrunk to a genteel suburban house he wasn't even needed to work for, and Jake had been caught by the inertia of change, both with the taproots of their women clinging to the defiled rock, making them stay" (343). Between them they demonstrate the easiest ways for a man in frontierless America to be defeated.

The central antagonists in the novel's drama are Hannah and her mother, who play out once again the endlessly repeated struggle between freedom and obedience. Part III of *The Killing Ground,* fittingly entitled "The Beginning," describes the funeral of Johnny McKarkle and the attempts by Hannah's mother to threaten and seduce her into remaining in Canona, a surrogate for the lost son. Plagued by headaches and nerves, Sally Brandon McKarkle is yet the most imposing figure of authority in the quintet after Cromwell, maybe the most imposing of all, since she combines the overt demands of a Cromwell with the wheedling dependency of her namesake, Sally Brandon Lacey, or Leah Catlett. "A monster of Southern respectability," she rearranges Hannah's life with the ease of a slave owner disposing of portable property.[14] Rather than offer advice, she commands: "Your father and I have made a decision and there's nothing you can do about it. You have to

14. Godwin, Review of *The Killing Ground,* 31.

face facts. *We can't afford* you anyplace but at home where you belong. And that is my last word" (338). The shift from "your father and I" to "my last word" reveals how little Hannah's father has actually had to say. Although Hannah tries to muster sympathy for her mother by remembering that "she has never in her life been asked to question" her ownership of other people (339), her descriptions of the woman customarily mix hatred, revulsion, and morbid curiosity: "She lay, spraddled, with the abandonment of a child. As we tiptoed in, she heaved her body over, away from us. She belched and buried her head in the pink pillow, legs spread and body flaccid under the ruffled tester of one of Egeria's Confederate beds, her defenses shed like clothes" (247). Caught unprepared and stripped of her "defenses," this southern monster appears childlike, vulnerable, ugly. Given the chance, however, "to take her own shape" and hide "the woman again behind the lady" (250), she becomes once more a figure of genteel, uncompromising power.

Hannah herself is the successor to Johnny Church, Jonathan Lacey, Johnny Catlett, and Lily Lacey, or alternately, given her fictional authorship of the previous novels, their model and creator. Her choice of (relative) poverty and isolation over claustrophobic subservience parallels "the no, or the failed no from Johnny Church who refused to doff his hat, through the demands of politics and circumstances on Jonathan Lacey, then the turning back to defeat of Johnny Catlett, through the escape to death of Lily" (399). Her combined sense of independence and abandonment is characteristically American, since "we were made of people who for three hundred years had left home because they had to, and who had had to carry with them that sense of loss" (356). What is not surprising, like Johnny Church and Lily Lacey (the figures with whom both Hannah and Settle seem to feel the closest kinship), she deliberately adopts Antigone as her spiritual forebear, calling Johnny McKarkle her "suburban Polynices" (154) and likening her homage to the dead and her subsequent punishment to the tragic heroine's. There is a danger here: because Hannah is the only protagonist conscious of her likeness to others in the quintet and of the archetypal nature of her own experiences, she is liable to appear to be playacting and, in Godwin's view, to be "overawed by her own Grand Design."[15] This con-

15. *Ibid.,* 30.

sciousness, however, exists not in the thirty-year-old Hannah enacting the rebellion but in the fifty-year-old Hannah recounting it, so though she eventually discovers that her moment of decision was part of a recurrent pattern, the moment itself is nonetheless terrifying and personal.

Even as Hannah undergoes a trial analogous to those of Johnny Church and Jonathan Lacey, the different nature of her experience illustrates one difference between early and contemporary America. Church's principled self-assertion means immediate death, Lacey's, a journey into the forbidden wilderness, but Hannah's choice means a scaled-down apartment and, as Settle puts it, having "everybody mad at you" (Appendix B, p. 164). Relatively small questions of form, relatively meaningless tests of obedience, are invested now with great significance because the momentous questions and tests have disappeared for all but a very few. Reasonably comfortable survival and the most basic freedoms are guaranteed for an educated, attractive, white American woman like Hannah; she must gauge success or failure, consequently, in terms that might have seemed trivial only a generation or two earlier. In *The Scapegoat,* I noted previously, only the women were confronted with genuinely exciting and dangerous choices, whereas most of the men felt trapped in impotent, diminished roles. By the time of *The Killing Ground,* the stakes for women and men seem comparably small, so that without much risk Hannah can do what for Lily would have been audacious. This change does not mean, paradoxically, that the contemporary characters in the quintet live more contentedly: if the price of freedom was dearer to premodern Americans, so were the tangible rewards, the differences between a life of liberty and a life of subservience, even a brief one, being immediately apparent. It takes Hannah twenty years and five books to recognize what, if anything, she has gained by her choice.

In the novel's brief epilogue, set in January of 1980, Hannah returns to Canona for the funeral of Aunt Althea Lacey. Wandering through the churchyard at Beulah, she manages both to collect the few missing pieces to the puzzle of Johnny McKarkle's death and, walking among the gravestones of Leah Cutwright, Johnny Catlett, and the rest, to look back over the fifteen hundred pages of the quintet. Aunt Althea, it turns out, had bailed Jake Catlett out of jail, persuaded Hannah's father to drop all charges, and provided Catlett with the money to begin a coal business that presently is thriving. With little explanation, simply a "This has gone far enough" (375), she had reasserted the importance of familial responsibility and ended a cycle of anger and retribution that stretched back three centuries. For Hannah the discovery seems cathartic: she acknowledges the end of her long, anxious search and considers with exquisite sympathy the ancestral graves stretched out across the hillside. Even her mother, "frightened, blindly running, dragging pride as a weapon and disguise" (381), she at last understands and forgives.

The setting and elegiac tone of the epilogue are fitting, for *The Killing Ground,* and in a more general way the entire quintet, may be seen as means of coming to terms with the dead. From its title to the three funerals around which it is structured to the recurrent image of Antigone and Polyneices, *The Killing Ground* is focused on the act of burial and particularly on the effects of the unburied dead on the living. Literally, it is the restless ghost of Johnny McKarkle, or for Settle the restless image of a nameless, fallen man, that accounts for the protracted search through history; figuratively, for nearly every character in the novel, it is the unburied past that haunts, often disfigures, and occasionally enriches the present. In staring at the graves of her ancestors and reading their epitaphs, Hannah performs directly the act performed metaphorically by the Beulah quintet and obliquely by many of its characters. She testifies, one final time, to the "stratum on stratum of connection" (384) between present and past.

Althea Lacey's "act of justice and love" is as meaningful and emblematic at the end of the quintet as was Johnny Church's act of separation at the beginning.[16] Almost imperceptibly, Althea evolves during the *The Scapegoat* and *The Killing Ground* from a flirtatious, sexually aggressive young woman to a drunken, middle-aged cynic to a matriarch of great power and compassion. Perhaps because she appears as a prominent character longer than anyone else in the quintet, these changes seem organic and inseparable from the history of the region. Having lived through the rebellions of her sister Lily and her niece Hannah, she recognizes the inevitability of such declarations of independence and can sympathize with parent and child; having experienced several

16. Garrett, *Understanding Mary Lee Settle,* 76.

reversals and rereversals in family fortune, she can discern the arbitrary, tenuous character of prosperity and the inseparability of oppressor and oppressed. She is, in effect, the Tiresias of the Beulah quintet, more prescient and universally empathic than any other character, and her redemption of Jake Catlett is an act of supreme historical and familial wisdom. She understands precisely how Catlett came to strike a drunken, well-dressed cousin in a jail cell and that a younger Hannah is in no position to share that understanding. To Hannah's complaint that Althea "never said a word" (375), the Catletts respond with the old aunt's wisdom:

> "Hannar, you can't never see but from where you stand. She wasn't about to tell you nothing."
> "Why?"
> "She didn't want to."
> That was all the explanation I had. . . .
> He unfolded himself from the car and came around to open my door. "She said they wasn't a bit of use in it," Loretta said from the back seat. (376)

Between the act of forgiveness and Hannah's discovery of it lies her writing of the Beulah novels and her development of the ability to understand its meaning and appropriateness. Only after creating Johnny Church, Jonathan Lacey, and the rest can she come to terms with the series of events that led to their creation.

Dominating the epilogue are Hannah's speculations about authorship in general and authoring the Beulah novels in particular. Some passages read nearly like an author's afterword: her recollection that "in a churchyard in England, [she] found the wall where Johnny Church and Thankful Perkins had been shot" (367) describes precisely the incident Settle has identified as the starting point of *Prisons* and "the most miraculous 'coincidence' of the whole quintet." In words nearly identical to Hannah's, Settle explains the novel's genesis: "I went with friends for a weekend in Burford, England, and I wandered into the churchyard and found bullet holes still in the churchyard wall where the real Johnny Church and Thankful Perkins were shot on April 14, 1649. Once again, I had found my book in a historic event, the refusal to fight in Ireland by several regiments of Cromwell's calvalry in 1649."[17]

17. Settle, "Search for Beulah Land," 24.

Hannah's confession that her initial attempt to "set down Johnny's death in words" had failed "because [she] knew too little of the past" (367) has been, again, Settle's own (Appendix B, p. 162). Generally Hannah's remarks echo those Settle has made in numerous interviews and articles during the past decade. Not surprising, this self-exegetical tendency has disturbed some readers of the novel, particularly since *The Killing Ground* invites comparison in so many other ways with modernist and postmodernist texts in which the author's perspective is concealed and few explicatory aids are provided. The feigned detachment of Joyce, more than the engagement of Dickens or George Eliot, has characterized most twentieth-century novels written in the complex manner of *The Killing Ground.* Here, however, the Joycean strategy simply would not work: Hannah, at the end, must demonstrate her own growth by revealing a newly mature understanding of her life and the fiction she has fashioned out of it—an understanding created by Settle that could be expected to resemble Settle's. This is merely to say that the reliable, first-person narrator of any autobiographical novel of development is likely to end by articulating moral, intellectual, and spiritual positions similar to the author's own. Since Hannah is not merely a character in but a creator of autobiographical fiction, her resemblance to the author is more than usually apparent.

Even at the end, though, the differences between Hannah and Settle are instructive. Because *The Killing Ground* is less an autobiographical novel than a novel about a novelist writing autobiography, it can be read as a meditation on the preferred relations between a writer's life and work. Hannah is closer to the material of the quintet than is Settle; its characters are her relatives and ancestors, its seminal incident, a turning point in her own history. For this reason her fiction, however lifelike, remains "a lie" until she establishes the "distance and empathy" (367) necessary to tell the story free of bias and resentment. As the collection of viewpoints in *The Scapegoat* and *The Killing Ground* demonstrates, history for Settle is more reliably seen from a variety of perspectives than from a single perspective, no matter how wise or well intentioned. For the novelist writing directly about the events of her own life, like Hannah, the movement from a personal to a communal point of view is liable to be especially difficult and to take place only after several failed attempts. The act of imaginatively re-creating history, that is, helps produce the capacity for "distance and empathy" necessary to re-create personal history without slipping into self-justification. Settle has made her own belief on this topic clear: "So many young writers start out by writing thinly disguised autobiography. I think you should end up with it, not begin with it."[18] The young novelist (and Hannah is more than a decade younger than Settle) is unlikely to make the crucial "intuitive jump" (Appendix B, p. 150) from raw material to fiction.

In at least one sense, Hannah ends by being a surrogate not just for the author but for the reader. Like the reader of the quintet, she has discovered in the past a group of recurrences, cycles, and types that enable her to contextualize and better understand events in the present. If she cannot change what she is or what her family and culture are, she can at least come to view her own situation less melodramatically and the behavior of those around her less resentfully. "History, by putting crisis in perspective," Arthur Schlesinger, Jr., has written, "supplies the antidote to every generation's illusion that its own problems are uniquely oppressive." The discovery that "rhythms, patterns, continuities" discernible in history continue "to mold the present and to color the shape of things to come" improves self-understanding and, presumably, the ability to anticipate the future.[19] Neither the ebb and flow between oppressor and oppressed nor the tension between Antigone and Creon will soon cease, no matter how comprehensively one studies history; but, as both Hannah McKarkle and Althea Lacey are meant to demonstrate, historical awareness can help soften the oppressor's blow and make the confrontation between Antigone and Creon less costly. For Settle, as for many historians, writing and reading about the past are acts of social and political consequence.

The initial published pages of the quintet describe Hannah Bridewell wandering lost through the woods of the Endless Mountains, entering for the first time the region where she and Jeremiah Catlett would found a family; the last pages describe Hannah McKarkle rising in a plane over the same woods and seeing for perhaps the final time the

18. *Contemporary Authors* (1980), 467.

19. Arthur Schlesinger, Jr., *The Cycles of American History* (Boston, 1986), xii–xiii.

"raw hills" that "rolled bluer and bluer in the distance" (383). The differences between the two landscapes measure the distance traveled during the intervening two centuries of American history: Beulah, not yet imagined in 1755, has been reduced in 1980 to the "flat white bandage of the [highway] ramp" (385), and the Catletts' hill farm has decayed into a "small wasteland" (385). The tangled wilderness that terrified the first Hannah, exploited by subsequent miners and developers, presents to the second "scars shining like battlements" and "new man-made tablelands pale among the skeletal winter trees" (383). The cycle has already begun again, however, and "patches of green" can be seen "where someone . . . had already begun the reclaiming of the land" (384). The river remains, as do the "clay and shale" that lie "like a sleeping giant" (383). For the last time, the contours of the valley are used to embody the mixture of stasis and change, or imperviousness and vulnerability to man, that comprises the historical process.

The contrast between the first and second Hannahs is even more telling. Hannah Bridewell, at the start in *O Beulah Land,* is the nearest thing in the quintet to a wholly isolated character: lost in the "black, left-alone nothing" (4), she can establish no connection with her environment or with another human being. Her point of view is narrowly focused and intensely subjective, her only concern, to satisfy the demands of hunger, thirst, and exhaustion. Hannah McKarkle, by contrast, has come to recognize "stratum on stratum of connection" among herself, the land, and "all the people that [she] had conjured up and brought to life again" (384). At the end she comes closer than any other character in the novels to a far-seeing objectivity free of bias and self-interest. Whereas Hannah Bridewell is trapped within the dense forest, unable to see far through the "selfish, high undergrowth" (5), the later Hannah literally rises above the landscape to see "mile after mile of mountains" (383). Both women, like nearly all Settle's protagonists, are "wanderers" driven by "an itch, a discontent, an unfulfilled promise" (384), and both pay a considerable price for having elected freedom. The later woman's awareness of history, however, enables her to replace the animal terror of her forebear with a calmer acceptance.

In the quintet's closing paragraph, Hannah drifts off to sleep, bringing to a finish the long narrative that began with the waking of Johnny Church in the Thames valley in 1649. She sleeps "between promise and hard pan as we"—the *we* meaning a particularly representative, independent American type—"always have" (385) and dreams a montage of images drawn from, yet finally unlike, her own life and fiction. "Tourists in blue Dacron" (385) and reconstructed houses mix with moonstones, witches, and fairies; in a tiny model of historical re-creation, the mundane is blended with the utterly imaginative to produce something familiar yet strange. In the novel's final line, "They all wore authentic sneakers and followed each other under the hill, and I was twenty and there was only Thankful Perkins to tell it to" (385), Hannah's voice modulates into the voice of Johnny Church to paraphrase the opening line, and call to mind the opening moment, of *Prisons*. The juxtaposition of start and finish reveals both the immense temporal and geographic distance covered by the narrative and the changeless nature of the individuals and issues with which it has from the beginning been concerned. The reader of the Beulah quintet ends, like Hannah, where he began, knowing the place for the first time.

# Conclusion

I began this book by noting the pointlessness of railing against the popular and academic marketplaces, which have both been unreceptive to the work of Mary Lee Settle. The forces that shape the best-seller lists and the canon are rarely argued into submission, and testimonies to the beauty, truth, and power of a text cannot easily be expanded into assertions that others should be similarly impressed with these qualities. Still, if one leaves aside questions of aesthetic and intellectual value, the Beulah quintet remains a work of considerable historical interest. Regardless, that is, of whether one considers the quintet great or theoretically important fiction, it is clearly distinctive fiction occupying a special place in American and contemporary literary history. And, like many anomalies, it casts into relief a number of the assumptions and restrictive impulses of the traditions from which, deliberately or not, it remains apart.

One might start with the fact that the quintet, when taken as a whole, is the longest work of serious fiction by an American woman. More than a mere curiosity, this distinction suggests, albeit obliquely, a good deal about the place of women in the history of the American novel and about the unusual character of Settle's novelistic ambitions. Unlike in England, where "women began to write respectable fiction near the end of the eighteenth century [and] became prominent novelists during the nineteenth," women in nineteenth-century America played a relatively peripheral role in the development of the serious novel.[1] This is not to say that there were few women novelists; in fact there were many. Nina Baym reports that novels written by women formed "by far the most popular literature of [the] time" and that "after the Civil War, the domination of the reading public by women became a fact that writers could ignore no longer."[2] Nor is it to say that novels written by women were uniformly second-rate; as David Reynolds has recently argued, nineteenth-century women's fiction has generally been "undervalued from a literary standpoint." Rather, it is merely to say that the kinds of novels customarily written by women were unlike those written by the major male novelists and influenced the formation of the canon and of highbrow critical taste only indirectly. What Baym defines as "woman's fiction"—fiction devoted to the sentimentalized representation of domestic life—"absorbed the full energies of almost all the women novelists in America for fifty years" while Cooper, Edgar Allan Poe, Hawthorne, and Melville were creating their most important works. In reading through these novels, Baym acknowledges, she did not unearth "a forgotten Jane Austen or George Eliot, or hit upon one novel that [she] would propose to set alongside *The Scarlet Letter.*" Harriet Beecher Stowe, as a major woman novelist of the time not writing so-called woman's fiction, Baym concedes to be the one major exception to the generalization. "One wishes," she writes, "that Stowe had tried her hand at the genre, partly because her gifts were substantial enough to have produced the truly major work that no writer in the genre achieved."[3] The contrast to the same period in England, which saw the publication of *Jane Eyre, Wuthering Heights, Middlemarch,* and *North and South,* is striking.

Several explanations for this transatlantic difference can be offered. Perhaps novels in the two countries tended to be written by different

1. Nancy Armstrong, *Desire and Domestic Fiction: A Political History of the Novel* (New York, 1987), 7.

2. Nina Baym, *Woman's Fiction: A Guide to Novels by and About Women in America, 1820–1870* (Ithaca, 1978), 11, 13. More recently, David Reynolds has called into question the accuracy of such claims, but even by his estimate the number of popular women novelists was substantial. See David S. Reynolds, *Beneath the American Renaissance: The Subversive Imagination in the Age of Emerson and Melville* (New York, 1988), 338–39.

3. Reynolds, *Beneath the American Renaissance,* 339; Baym, *Woman's Fiction,* 13, 14, 16.

sorts of women. In England, Nancy Armstrong notes, the major women writers were usually "intellectuals" who "can be seen to take the virtues embodied by the domestic woman and to pit them against working-class culture." In America, by contrast, women novelists "saw themselves not as 'artists' but as professional writers with work to do and a living to be made from satisfactory fulfillment of an obligation to their audience." Perhaps, as Ann Douglas has argued, "nineteenth-century America was, in certain senses . . . usually considered pejorative, more Victorian than other countries to whom the term is applied," more even than Victorian England, and therefore less receptive to challenging, overtly intellectual women like George Eliot and Charlotte Brontë.[4] Although these broad (and admittedly imperfect) distinctions may be valid, however, they seem to me more symptomatic than explanatory. American women novelists conceived of themselves differently, wrote different books, and met with a different audience because nineteenth-century America imagined itself differently than did England or any other country in nineteenth-century Europe.

The same urge to mythologize that shaped American historical fiction virtually guaranteed that American women novelists of the nineteenth century would be marginalized, for, as Judith Fryer points out, the controlling myth "envisioned by our poets and philosophers, by our seers and reformers, and especially by our novelists, [was] the myth of the New World Adam." And "if Eve was the cause of the original Adam's downfall, the role of the New World Eve must be minimized." Female characters play comparatively small roles in the major novels of the American Renaissance. Moreover, because writers like Cooper, Hawthorne, Thoreau, Melville, and Walt Whitman "turned their sights principally on values and scenes that operated as alternatives to cultural norms," the sorts of domestic experience available to most women were unlikely to form the stuff of serious literature.[5] American women, that is, were excluded from the central tradition of the novel not by inclination or ability but by setting, plot, and theme, in the same way that certain types of documentary truth, particularly about colonization,

4. Armstrong, *Desire and Domestic Fiction,* 8; Baym, *Woman's Fiction,* 16; Ann Douglas, *The Feminization of American Culture* (New York, 1977), 5.

5. Judith Fryer, *The Faces of Eve: Women in the Nineteenth-Century American Novel* (New York, 1976), 6; Douglas, *Feminization of American Culture,* 5.

were excluded from American historical fiction. In England, conversely, the traditions of realism and social reform, which attempt to confront rather than escape Victorianism and draw naturally on the characteristic experiences of both men and women, enabled Dickens and George Eliot, Thackeray and Charlotte Brontë, to write fiction of roughly the same kind.

Although women have played a much more prominent role in the development of the American novel since the late nineteenth century, certain traces of their earlier exclusion and of the dominance of the Edenic myth remain. The most influential women novelists of this century have for the most part written realistic and domestic fiction; the epic and historical tradition, while becoming less central, has remained predominantly male. Faulkner, Dos Passos, Barth, and Mailer write fiction of dramatically different kinds, but they are kinds that tend not to be written by women and tend to reinforce, in one way or another, many of the mythic assumptions of the nineteenth century. The grandly ambitious, panoramic study attempted by Settle, which consciously engages the development of American culture and represents equally the experience of men and women, frontier and drawing room, has few antecedents in the history of American women's fiction. Reviewers, ignoring the fact of her novels, may have classified her as a writer of popular historical romance because that is the only kind of historical fiction customarily written by women.

To invoke again a comparison made earlier, Settle bears roughly the relation to the ideas and expectations of her age and culture that George Eliot did to hers a century before. Like Settle, Eliot was a pioneer who wrote novels that many of her contemporaries considered intellectually and even formally masculine; though women were expected to write fiction, they were not expected to write the kind Eliot favored. More than, say, Jane Austen or Charlotte Brontë, Eliot attempted to represent male and female experience equally and a broad range of social and economic conditions. Jennifer Uglow might be describing Settle's fiction when she calls Eliot's work "rich in a marvelously observed range of portraits of both men and women, including an often neglected group of women who exercise considerable power (for good or ill) in customary or traditional domestic spheres." Also like Settle, Eliot stood in her own day, and to a degree still stands, in somewhat uneasy relation to feminism, since her concern was less to foreground female experience or erase distinctions between men and women than to reveal the complex interactions between male and female tendencies, with the ultimate hope, perhaps, of "feminizing" men and "masculinizing" women. Both novelists actively avoided categorization as writers of women's fiction: Settle has said, with approval, "You cannot call me a women's novelist" (Appendix B, p. 154), and Eliot, in her parodic attack on "Silly Novels by Lady Novelists," termed such writers "inexperienced in every form of poverty except poverty of brains."[6]

In order to force entry into a largely masculine tradition and to redefine the place of women in the American past, Settle has had to reconceptualize the history and distinguishing characteristics of America. One way of putting this is to say that she has attempted to create a new, more androgynous American myth, replacing the myth of the New World Adam with that of Antigone and Creon. In her version the roles of both principals may be played by either men or women, and the peculiar challenges, restrictions, and promises of America are not limited to the customary spheres of either sex. Cultural restraints of course affect the likelihood that women would occupy the rebellious or domineering roles. During the eighteenth and nineteenth centuries, women had comparatively few opportunities openly to challenge authority; during much of the twentieth century, Settle seems to imply, women may have had more, or at least more interesting, opportunities than men. But the central myth, unlike the Edenic one, is neither sexually defined nor exclusionary. America is imagined not as the place where men are perpetually creating a new, more perfect world without or even despite women but as the place where the demands of freedom and obedience are perpetually in a condition of tension. The latter myth not only incorporates women, non-Anglo immigrants, and others excluded from the Edenic one but helps account for their experiences in the New World.

Settle's American myth, again unlike the Edenic one, is founded on an engagement with rather than an avoidance or selective recollection of history (what meaningful history, after all, could have preceded the formation of Eden?). Given the scarcity of instructive American mod-

6. Jennifer Uglow, *George Eliot* (New York, 1987), 3; Eliot, *Essays,* 304.

els, it is not surprising that she turned to the European novel to find helpful examples of imaginative history, forming a hybrid between American and European traditions of historical fiction analogous to that formed by Henry James in the novel of manners. Depending on one's point of view, James either Americanized the European novel or Europeanized the American; Settle brought to the European historical novel an American emphasis on freedom and change, to the American, a European emphasis on factual integrity. The resulting work, ironically, stands outside or on the fringes of either tradition (again, I would argue, like the novels of James) because it is so obviously informed by both.

During the past two or three decades, serious historical fiction has been making something of a comeback on both sides of the Atlantic, at least to the extent that a historical novelist today can be placed into a reasonably broad contemporary context. Settle can be said to have anticipated this resurgence by ten or fifteen years, though, to be honest, probably not to have caused or substantially influenced it. The increasingly visible literatures of Latin America and Asia more than the traditions of North America and Europe, I suspect, are responsible for the renewed interest in panoramic or mythic historical fiction. The result has been many fine but few distinctively American novels—few, that is, deeply rooted in the language, customs, and political ideology of America. Settle's way of imagining the past is meant to be characteristically American in the sense that Gabriel García Márquez' is meant to be Colombian or Milan Kundera's Czechoslovakian. She shares with many writers of the Third World especially a passion for understanding the formation of her national culture, perhaps because, in her view, America is by definition a perpetually emerging nation.

George Eliot, Henry James, and Gabriel García Márquez are heady company, and clearly I have been making by implication, if not by direct argument, some rather lofty claims for the stature of the Beulah quintet. I have been succumbing, that is, to precisely the universal urge I began by identifying and, so far as was possible, dismissing—the urge to demonstrate the historical and aesthetic importance of my subject and to justify thereby my own critical enterprise. Although surely self-serving and possibly ineffectual, this urge is nonetheless unavoidable. Ultimately one reads books in the hope of discovering something of personal value and writes about books in the effort to share the discovery of value with others. The arguments about Settle's complex adaptations of tradition, sophisticated response to history, and formal originality are, like most criticism, various ways of explaining and supporting an assertion considerably more elemental: the novels that comprise the Beulah quintet are simply too valuable to be overlooked.

# Appendix A
## A Selective Genealogy

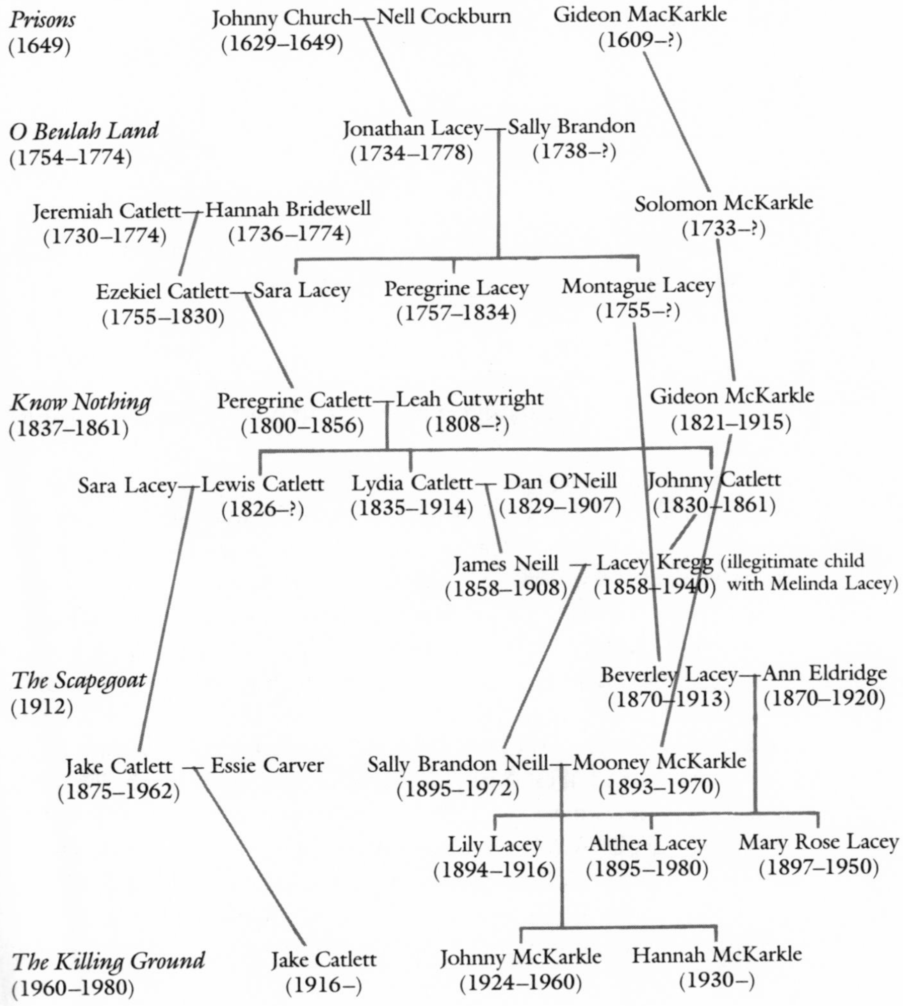

# Appendix B
## An Interview with Mary Lee Settle

*The following transcript is drawn from conversations held in Charlottesville, Virginia, in June of 1987.*

**BR:** During an interview several years ago, you suggested that too many "young writers start out by writing thinly disguised autobiography" and that a writer "should end up with it, not begin with it." Could you explain?

**MLS:** I think that's so important. I start every lecture I give by saying that there's been a fashion that has totally misled young writers, and that is "write about what you know," because you know screw-all. Unless you dip very, very deep into the raw material that you're going to use, you never make the intuitive jump from raw material to fiction. Fiction didn't happen. It's that simple. It isn't something that happened with the names changed. It didn't happen. I mean, it may be based on something that happened, but a good fiction writer will transmute raw material. Say, a man is walking down the street; it's noon; it's a hot day in a small town in West Virginia. He stumbles at the curb. This is a memory. The fact that a Rolls Royce hits him and he sues moves into fiction. The Rolls Royce may have been somewhere else, the lawsuit may have been somewhere else, but that amalgam has to happen in the writer's mind by a kind of alchemy. The raw material of fiction is often one's personal life, but it is also one's reading, one's observance, everything.

**BR:** How about the second part of your remark, that you should end up with autobiography. Is that something you envision yourself doing at some point?

**MLS:** Yes, I'm doing it right now. I'm writing almost total autobiography. But it gets loose from me even so because I'm so used to writing fiction now, and even in a totally nonfictional recall I find myself conjuring and spinning. But then, you can go back and write books that on the surface seem far from autobiography and discover you have been doing the opposite. I look back on my work and see autobiographical fragments all the way through it.

**BR:** Do you see those in any particular book or character with special clarity?

**MLS:** Yes. Somebody asked me that before, expecting me to say the second Hannah, who is not autobiographical at all.

**BR:** But when you're a woman novelist writing about a woman novelist, those kinds of connections are going to suggest themselves.

**MLS:** Yes, but the better connection is the psychic one of the real identification. Dickens said he had in his heart of hearts a favorite child, and his name was David Copperfield. I have in my heart of hearts a favorite identity, and it's Johnny Church. That tension between Puritanism and the Cavalier gesture is a basic American dilemma. It's a dilemma that goes through all five volumes.

**BR:** Is that why, in the last line of the quintet, you come back to Johnny?

**MLS:** You know, when I got to that, I just stopped writing and I fell apart. I realized that it had taken twenty-eight years and I had gone full circle finally.

**BR:** Let me try another quotation. When you accepted the National Book Award in 1978, you spoke of "an unnamed but recognized quality inherent in good work." Can you describe in any sense what this quality consists in for you?

**MLS:** I think you recognize it. Words stop being words and become a reality of their own. You find it in Hopkins' poetry. You know, suddenly it just soars. You find it in "Typhoon," when the man comes on deck in the storm and then the room is completely still, the cabin is still, and suddenly the stars run down the heavens. I mean, God, it's not words anymore.

**BR:** It's language that makes you forget it's language?

**MLS:** That's right. It disappears into the scene.

**BR:** What novelists do you read?

**MLS:** I'm like Gerald Ford: I can't read and write at the same time.

**BR:** Do you stop reading other novelists while you're working on a book?

**MLS:** Oh, God, yes, because I've too keen an ear. It scares me how easily I could pick up stylistic tricks. I read in between books, except I have been working so much I haven't had a chance to do it this time. I'll read a whole favorite writer just for the pure pleasure of it. All of Conrad, who is my favorite, my "grandfather." And Hardy. I tend to like nineteenth-century novels. Some twentieth-century. I've read Proust over and over again. *Maison Rendezvous* of Robbe-Grillet to me is a model for what I'm working on now. The almost unbearable intensity in that book is just marvelous. But a lot of times what you learn from isn't necessarily what you like especially. I would have to avoid every one of those when I am working, lest I imitate them.

**BR:** The Conrad connection seems particularly strong; as you say, you've called him your "chosen psychic grandfather." Can you enlarge on that a bit?

**MLS:** Well, in the first place I think the kind of logical positivist view of the English language is bullshit. We are just two steps beyond hog calling anyway, struggling for language all the time. And here was Conrad, who had of course a deep Shakespearean background, which I identify with, but it was in Polish; he did not learn English until he was nineteen years old. He came to the language new, which is the way we should all come to the language. Just that sense of its miracle I think you get so strongly in Conrad. He tried as clearly as he could to keep up a kind of infinite questioning, to say the unsayable. Time after time in Conrad, we find not an easy-going suburban ease of writing and subject but a real struggle to say something that is hard to articulate and understand.

**BR:** I also sense that the way Conrad tells a story might appeal to you. The narrator suggests in *Heart of Darkness* that the truth of a story may not be in a kernel at the center but hovering around the edges like a misty halo.

**MLS:** Well, maybe I was affected in that way, but I think the real charm was to get me to question a little more, work a little harder, dive a little deeper. If he could do it, I could do it. I once said to a friend of mine that I wanted to question beyond Pavese and not commit suicide.

**BR:** A number of European writers have been talked about in connection with your work. Malcolm Cowley referred to the Tolstoyan and the Proustian aspects of your fiction and also to the fact that these aspects may at times come into conflict with one another. Do you see yourself as having ties, particularly in your historical novels, to either writer?

**MLS:** Yes, though only after the fact. Set this five-volume book up against another huge book, *War and Peace*. That mixture of the personal and eventual is like Tolstoy. The canvas is big, like Tolstoy's. The intimacies are there, maybe like Proust.

**BR:** Maybe this is the tension Cowley was talking about. You're trying to give the quintet a Tolstoyan breadth yet to look at moments with the leisure and specificity of Proust.

**MLS:** It's necessary. I think what's wrong with *War and Peace* is that it's always either/or. The battle where Prince Andrei is wounded and the bodies of the officers and the men are seen in different colors is a wonderful scene. It's individual, even though it's in a huge canvas. But then Tolstoy cheated in the worst Cecil B. DeMille way at the Battle of Borodino. What does he do? He has Pierre wandering around. I mean, come on. That was disgraceful of Tolstoy. He'd been in battles. He knew better than that.

**BR:** But hasn't this always been the problem writers of historical fiction have had? On the one hand, they're trying to capture these important historical moments, these grand historical events, yet on the other, they're trying to give one a sense of commonplace experience at the time.

**MLS:** Right. Nobody did it better than Stephen Crane in *The Red Badge of Courage,* where there's all the intensity of the battle and then the other soldiers come by and say this wasn't the battle, the battle was over there.

**BR:** Jumping from Tolstoy to Crane seems to suggest that your own work relates to a number of different literary traditions. Do you see yourself, for instance, as in any way a distinctly American novelist? Does such a category even exist for you?

**MLS:** Not for me. Essentially I began to write with a European sensibility. Although there are American works and European works, to me they're all the same. I don't care what county you write about, whether the county is Surrey or Albemarle.

**BR:** Of course, critics and historians like to categorize.

**MLS:** Well, sure. It's so easy.

**BR:** What about feminist fiction? Do you see women's novels as forming a definable category?

**MLS:** Some of them. I think I call them vaginal novels. There are some novels, and they're not very good, that set out to be women's novels. But there can be novels about women, written by women, that are not women's novels: *Middlemarch, The Age of Innocence*, or *The House of Mirth*. And there are some fine women's novel novelists, who I'm sure were not aware of or interested in such a category. Colette, for instance, is one. Her novels smell of bedrooms, talcum powder, and scent.

**BR:** Do you think that one of the reasons your work hasn't been more widely read is precisely because you are very difficult to categorize?

**MLS:** I think that's absolutely true. You cannot call me a southern novelist; you cannot call me a women's novelist. I like that.

**BR:** You also may be unfashionable in your placement of tremendous importance on the faithfulness of what you write, on its truth to what actually is.

**MLS:** I think it would be terrible to write and not to. The work's too hard not to tell the truth, as nearly as you can. It may be a *Rashomon* kind of attempt at truth, but often that's the reason, not any literary reason, that people tell a story.

**BR:** Is this one of the reasons you've written historical fiction, because you have this skeleton of truth, or seed of truth, around which to build the fiction?

**MLS:** No, I didn't have it. I was trying to find it. I kept trying to find it and trying to find it and that's why I think *Prisons* is such an important book.

**BR:** You've described the seed of the quintet as the image of a man's fist hitting another man's face in a drunk tank. Does that have any particular source?

**MLS:** No.

**BR:** It turned out to be the impetus for five books.

**MLS:** I don't know what the source of it was. I have never started writing a book without a concrete image. The image doesn't even need to be important. For instance, in *Blood Tie* I saw a lipstick lying on the sea floor forty meters down. It was the first image I had. It was out of that image that the whole of *Blood Tie* came. What was the lipstick doing on the sea floor? Actually, you don't see the lipstick on the sea floor until right at the end of the book. Johnny Church I saw killed, but that was true because I went into the churchyard where it happened. The man hitting the other man in the drunk tank, I just *saw* it that way.

**BR:** George Garrett has referred to all of your novels, not just those in the quintet, as chapters or units of one larger design. Would you agree?

**MLS:** I think somebody else has to see that. Consciously, of course, I didn't do it that way.

**BR:** Naturally, it's the kind of statement that one can make about most writers who produce a substantial body of work into which they put a lot of themselves. But I sense from Garrett's comment that he sees it as being more true of you than of most others.

**MLS:** There are all kinds of connections.

**BR:** Thinking back over the novels you've produced to this point, do you notice any consistent changes, any things that you find have happened over nearly four decades?

**MLS:** There's a lot more compassion now. *The Love Eaters* is a mean book.

**BR:** It's sustained irony of the kind you find in Conrad.

**MLS:** Wasn't I lucky to get over my irony early? You know, you think of Conrad and you think of Twain and you think of all these people, Goya as a painter, they all ended up in a state of horror at the world. I seem to have started out that way.

**BR:** Your first two novels are almost the sort one would expect from a writer who had been working for years and become jaded. You've gone in the opposite direction.

**MLS:** I was teased in Paris when *The Love Eaters* came out. Oh, people said, you're going to end up writing *Rebecca of Sunnybrook Farm.* Well, of course, I didn't. *Celebration* is far from that. But it is very affirmative.

**BR:** Any other changes?

**MLS:** Well, you know, I am nearly blind in one eye, and I started out as a writer who was so aural. I was writing plays. I wasn't seeing. And I really forced myself to learn to see, and of course now the books have become so visual. I remember that I got some idea that because I couldn't see out of my left eye, part of my brain wasn't being used. So I was down in Cornwall, and I got a big piece of art paper and a piece of charcoal about so thick, and I was going to create a memory. So I put a patch over my good eye, and I would turn around and I would look. As a result of doing this for a long time, I can now see my separate fingers move and I can see all the colors, though I can't focus on them. Anyway, I would turn around and I would look at a mountain or a hill and then down into the sea, and I would slowly turn around again, close my eyes, and remember the mountain; and then I would draw it. And of course what I was drawing looked like the drawing of a drunken child, but I still was having a mental lag between vision and recollection. I was training myself to see.

**BR:** I'd like to focus now on the historical fiction more directly and in doing so to raise a question about the category itself. You've said elsewhere that you don't like to make a distinction between your historical and contemporary novels. But is this actually true? Do you find you can't make distinctions?

**MLS:** Let me explain what I meant by that. Anything that happens in the past, even if it's in your own personal past, becomes history at once. The gulf is whether it's in your lifetime or not.

**BR:** Is this how you distinguish between historical and contemporary novels?

**MLS:** That's right. For instance, *The Charterhouse of Parma* is not a historical novel. Parts of *War and Peace* are not because Tolstoy was alive. But even before your own lifetime, you have historic memory, even more than historic memory, historic familiarity, which can reach back through family and cultural inheritance. But your own historic memory and your communal historic memory sometimes are as false as your personal memory and always need checking. We're in the South right now, and the historic memory of the South goes back beyond the Civil War, but it's a false memory because it's all glossed over with nostalgia and excuses and so on. So, when you're writing history, you have to cut through the communal memory in the way you cut through your personal memory when you're trying to tell the truth. On the other hand, you can go back so far, and I did in both *O Beulah Land* and *Prisons,* that you have to create a memory. I did it in both cases by doing a great deal of reading without taking any notes. It's just like people who are illiterate often have much better memories because they have to remember. For *O Beulah Land* I read for about ten months before I took a single note because I needed to create an ambience of memory, and then a wonderful night happened when I dreamed about putting up a small shack in order to make a claim on forty acres of land. I knew then that I had a memory. What I really meant before was that technically—no, not technically, I hate that word because it's an intellectual word—in the vision or the dream I begin with, I never have felt any difference between a vision in contemporary space and a vision in historic time. One's as real for me as the other.

**BR:** George Eliot wrote, over a century ago, that imaginative history was the most important kind of writing one could do. Would you agree?

**MLS:** I would agree so strongly that when I was beginning to try to find out why the man hit the other man in the drunk tank, I thought of writing social history, and I realized that social history wouldn't do. You have to put yourself back there and become contemporary with it in order to understand. And that's spoken as a writer. If the writer is good, then the reader becomes contemporary with the time of the book. For instance, you are reading *Prisons* in the twentieth century, but the sense of immediacy should be strong enough so you think that Johnny and Thankful have lost their lives for nothing. It takes a certain intellectual jump to realize that you're sitting here and you're speaking English and you're in a democracy and even "them poor benighted Catholics" are voting, to say nothing of women, because of men like Johnny and Thankful, who thought they were failures. See what I'm getting at? It's a sort of double thing, isn't it? You leave the present, and then you come back into the present with a psychic and emotional knowledge. I think that's what George Eliot meant.

**BR:** You mention rejecting the idea of writing social history. In a piece you wrote a few years ago for the *New York Times Book Review,* you made a distinction again between the historian and the historical novelist. How, in fact, do you distinguish between the two?

**MLS:** Fiction didn't happen.

**BR:** Don't historians create fictions, too? Don't they construct narratives?

**MLS:** Yes. But narrative is not necessarily fiction. Have you read Shelby Foote's three-volume *Civil War?* It's a brilliant book. It's one of the great American books, I think. He has that balance between narrative and anecdote which English historians have at their best. Where I can go beyond historic narrative is that I can go into the mind of Jonathan Lacey, who is watching a ford on the Monongahela River and who has just written to his wife to tell her what the land is like. Do you see the difference? It's the freedom of being able to create a person who may reflect the time and whom you can empathize with.

But the thing that the good historical fiction writer shares with the good historian is that neither screws around with the facts. When Johnny Church joined the English Parliamentary army, you'll remember, he sees it first from a hill, looking down at the Roundheads. That's where they were that day in 1645; Cromwell was there. When they went north to Naseby, Cromwell did turn up that night before. All of that is documented. In other words, I could mess around with fictional characters but not with life as it happened.

**BR:** You feel that you have as a novelist the freedom to extrapolate from the facts but not to alter or ignore the facts.

**MLS:** Right, because basically you're going to fail. You weren't there. But the least failure is to become empathetic with the times. I had some terrible problems with this, by the way. Because you can't write down characters without having a strong empathy for them. You cannot do it. A person is dead on the page if you do. And I don't care what capabilities you have to draw out of yourself. This goes back to what we were talking about, people writing about what they know. You've experienced all the emotions. All you have to do is find them. You have to have empathy with the murderer at the right point. Dostoevsky did this with Raskolnikov. Goethe said, "I, myself, am capable of every crime."

**BR:** Did you have any particular problems identifying with any single character, with Cromwell, for instance?

**MLS:** No, I felt sorry for Cromwell. I found a kind of interior softness in Cromwell; it was those droopy eyes of his, you know.

**BR:** What, for your purposes in these novels, is history? Is it anything that happened in the past?

**MLS:** No. The kind of pulsing line of history in this book is the history of people who caused some essential social change despite their belief that they'd failed. All the way through the book, there's a series of pitch points at which the world changes, and there is no way to go back to a world before they happened. It's almost a definition of revolution. That's why I wasn't interested in writing about the actual American Revolution or the Civil War or whatever and only touched the First World War. What I'm interested in is the seed. Whether it's the seed of failure or the seed of success, it's the seed of change. You watch it planted.

**BR:** Let me throw another term at you, one you've used before. You once said that you knew you'd been told myths as a child and have always distrusted them. How do you distinguish between those myths and what historians and novelists and most of us call history?

**MLS:** The difference is to go back and find out what actually happened. The difference is between reading a letter written by Aunt Essie when she was a young girl going to a ball in 1855 and listening to a story told by lovely old Aunt Essie's daughter about her mother going to the same ball, in 1930: when you're a child, your ears are big.

**BR:** Isn't much of what we casually call history really myth? Look at the schoolbooks through the years that have taught us American history. Hasn't it as often been American myth?

**MLS:** Well, it's American myth, and it's American censorship. Remember the so-called Battle of Point Pleasant, which was just a massacre? You pick up any history book, and it will tell you about Cornstalk and the Battle of Point Pleasant. God, I even went into a bar up in Warm Springs and it was called the Simon Kenton Bar, and I said I don't want to stay in a bar named after that murderous bastard. To most of the people he was his myth, not his reality.

**BR:** History, you mean, is true; myth is what people want to have happened?

**MLS:** It can, of course, be archetypal and represent a truth, or it can be a mixture of nostalgia and forgetting. Some myths *are* wonderful, you know. Was it John Ford who said that if you have to make a choice between the fact and the myth, print the myth? But when the fallible human being is simplified into the archetype, the myth can be dangerous. You know the myth of Cupid and Psyche is psychically true; Scarlett and Rhett are not. *Myth* is such a funny word, anyway. Myth can be psychically true, and at the same time it can be a cover-up for the past. We've lost a lot of people in the past. Nobody, including myself, knew who Freeborn Jack Lilburne was. All I knew was that Thomas Jefferson had the name *Lilburne* on a ring. I even asked Dumas Malone, and he was vague about it and said he thought it was a family name. Family name, hell. Lilburne was the leader of the Levellers, and the Leveller language of democracy is a source of much of what Jefferson believed in.

**BR:** Why did you begin writing historical fiction at a time when it was in most respects out of fashion?

**MLS:** I wasn't concerned with that. You write what you have to write. It's just one long fight between Jacob and the Angel.

**BR:** Still, you must be aware that historical fiction has, at least in this century, had to fight an ongoing battle for acceptance.

**MLS:** Of course. It's generally thought of as what I call "tits across the Alleghenies," or the Mammary School of historical writing.

**BR:** Do you believe it's because the form has been used and abused so often by pulp novelists that serious novelists who turn to it have had to fight this battle?

**MLS:** I think that's absolutely true. What tickles me is that when I began, I was an acerbic young novelist getting a great deal of praise, and suddenly I was writing a historical novel. The noses turned up all over the place, and I lost what reputation I was building. Mind you now, I must be fair, *O Beulah Land* was extremely well received, and it has very seldom been out of print since 1956. But still, the literary snobs and politicians thought I had made a terrible mistake. I remember people saying to me, "You just can't do that." You know, "You'll ruin your reputation," and "It's such a debased genre" and all that. My answer was: "I can't help it if my book stretches that far back into the past. I have to do it."

You know, it just struck me. One of the differences between the historian and the person who's going to write imaginatively about history is that you become a kind of psychic and sensuous archaeologist. The smell, the touch of a certain cloth, the pace of a city: all of that you have to become familiar with. The historian isn't necessarily concerned with how a kid glove feels on a hand, you know. And you don't set out to discover these things. You simply find you need to know.

**BR:** It appears as if serious historical fiction has become relatively popular once again.

**MLS:** I really do think you work in an atmosphere of acceptance, whether you know you're doing it or not. And frankly, I busted out of the atmosphere of acceptance for *O Beulah Land* simply because the force of having to know was stronger. That's all.

**BR:** The Beulah quintet actually began as a trilogy. Did you always plan on expanding the initial three novels into a longer sequence, or was that a decision made later?

**MLS:** I'll tell you when the decision was made, and it was made very sloppily. I finished things too quickly with *Fight Night on a Sweet Saturday.* It was a failure, and one of the reasons it was a failure was that Viking insisted that I take out the 1907 section, which was just a short section with the mother as a girl. It happened to be a time, 1963 or 1964, when, like now, criticism was smart-alecky, and I got very, very bad reviews for *Fight Night*. I was upset by it, but I put it away because I was already at work on *All the Brave Promises*. Then I wrote *The Clam Shell.* And then, in order to get back to England, I wrote a book called *The Scopes Trial* in five weekends, and one of the things I found out was the motto of the American Civil Liberties Union, which is from John Lilburne's speech in 1632, and something clicked in my head. I thought, well, the trilogy's a failure. You know, I just had to live with that. But one of the reasons that I thought it was a failure . . . well, I had two reasons. One was that it had started too late. Jefferson said, "Why should I have to go back to Moses to find out what God said to Jean-Jacques Rousseau?" Well, I found out I wasn't quite near enough to Moses. I knew about land hunger. But our language, our language of democracy, I still hadn't found. And suddenly, here was the motto of the American Civil Liberties Union: "What is done to one man is done to all men." And my mind began going, and I thought, God, I wonder if somehow our political language is a result of a failed revolution? I never intended to write about it, but I thought, well, I must find out what the background of the people in *O Beulah Land* was. And I found Johnny and Thankful, literally. I found the wall where they were shot. And this is the reason for *Prisons*.

Now, obviously, it was going to be a quartet instead of a trilogy. So after *The Clam Shell* was finished, I went to a Greek island and started to work on *Prisons*. I took a bunch of tapes I had made of the language of Cromwell and the Putney debates, and I took some books. I had lived a year in Oxford and London doing research, so I was ready to write. And walking down the street one day, I heard two college students talking, two Englishmen. I ran up to one of them and said, "Are you from East Anglia?" He said yes. I said, "Will you do me a favor? Would you read something into a tape for me?" I had him read two of Cromwell's speeches during the Putney debates just to get that vowel sound from the Fens, which has never changed, you know. And so then there was *Prisons* and there were four of them, and I still was bothered because how can you write about coal country without writing about the mine wars? Then I went and wrote *Blood Tie,* but it still kept niggling at me and I couldn't let the angel go, and so I realized that the whole thing was not yet complete, that one of the reasons for the failure of *Fight Night on a Sweet Saturday* was that I didn't know enough about their parents. So it became kind of pathetic. Twenty years ago, I had found a five-thousand-page transcript of a 1913 Senate investigation into the Holly Grove massacre. Of course, this was all taken down in shorthand and printed verbatim. And I thought, there's my language and somewhere in there is my story, the one that would show what the mine wars were like. Then suddenly I saw the parents of Hannah and Johnny. There they were, all of them, as young people; so they gave a depth to the later story. The resonances from Althea, from Jake Catlett's daddy, from all of them in *The Scapegoat,* give the later characters a reason for being and give you an understanding you didn't have before. Then I used *Fight Night* as a kind of kernel of *The Killing Ground,* and that's how it grew into a quintet. Not a decision to write five instead of three but just another one and another one.

**BR:** Do you envision the novels of the quintet as parts of a long whole or as separate works that connect in important ways?

**MLS:** To me it is one book. It is absolutely one.

**BR:** So each of the later novels is better if you have read the earlier ones.

**MLS:** Yes, you get the echo. Because one of the themes of the book is that we know more about the past than the people who were living in it knew when it was the present. One of the things I had to do was go back and become so contemporary in mind with them that I had no sense of future and could describe not what was happening but what people thought was happening at the time. This was creating their culture. And especially before the Civil War, what people thought was happening was sometimes very far from what was actually happening.

**BR:** Why have you tried to write each of these novels in the language of the period in which it's set?

**MLS:** Oh, I think it's of essential importance, because language changes, and the language you're using at the time reflects the time so strongly, you know. The hardest language I had to deal with was in *Prisons,* because written language was very formal, and then fortunately I found the *Thomason Tracts,* a series of broadsheets collected during the English civil wars, where they just took stuff down in shorthand, printed it in a basement, and sold it in the street, no editing, no anything. So it was heard language. The language of a time reflects as much as the architecture or the clothes what the time is like. For instance, the whole sense of biblical language in the mid-seventeenth century was because of the Puritans. Well, you can't oversimplify and say it was only the Puritans, but the ambience of language was a new religious ambience. It had only been thirty years since the King James version of the Bible, if that. I mean, this was a new book! This was the way people talked. In the eighteenth century, because of the whole Roman revival, there was a Roman structure to sentences. There was a concern with Latin. Every educated man knew Latin. And even in the compliments and the slang, you could tell what people were thinking about. To call somebody facetious in the eighteenth century was a great compliment: it meant to be witty, facile. To say somebody was a heavy-bottomed man now would mean he's fat. Then it meant a solid, four-square fellow, you know, dependable. *Libertine* in the mid-seventeenth century meant literally a liberal. Then it began to take on a sexual connotation. So you see, if you don't know the language, how can you know the people? The changes in English are as profound to me as a change from French to Italian. The language of *Know Nothing* was a very self-consciously romantic language: a lot of four-syllable words, you know, very "little finger in the air" kind of language. There was a reaction among certain aristocratic men who wouldn't be caught dead saying "isn't" instead of "ain't," you know, who dropped their *g*'s, as they had learned from their parents and grandparents. Eighteenth-century gentlemen dropped their *g*'s. They said "ain't." Their vowel sounds were slightly different. So you meet somebody in the mid-nineteenth century who says "janeral" instead of "general," and you know something about his class, whether he's a countryman, and so forth. All these things are so profoundly important.

**BR:** Do you think you managed this linguistic re-creation particularly well in any one of the books?

**MLS:** I think Johnny Church's language in *Prisons* is very successful, because that was a very subtle transitional language. For instance, Johnny says "you" instead of "thee," which puts him in one particular social and educational category.

**BR:** Beginning in *Prisons* and continuing all the way through the quintet, you seem to focus on what you call at the end the "price of freedom." What exactly is the price one pays for being free?

**MLS:** I can trace it through the whole quintet. Johnny Church's price of freedom is to die. Jonathan Lacey has to go over into the King's Part, west of the Alleghenies; he has to disobey the law. In *Know Nothing* Johnny Catlett fails. He doesn't pay the price of freedom. The result is, and, God, this reverberates so, we have a Civil War. In other words, that failure to pay was embodied in *Know Nothing* in one person's decision when it was the decision of thousands. Lily frees herself in *The Scapegoat,* only to die. And in *The Killing Ground,* to ask for freedom in the culture that we come from is painful. You remember Johnny Church says we must accept as hallowed the unblessing of our fathers. There's an awful prisonlike fraud that I think we create very strongly in this country. Maybe we have to be so dependent on family because we don't have much communal sense, especially with the huge immigrations that clutch together, you know. Maybe that's what it is. I don't know. The price of freedom is to have everybody mad at you. That's putting it down at its lowest, and most understandable, everyday reaction.

**BR:** More than once in the quintet you draw on the myth of Antigone and Creon to embody the tensions you're talking about. Clearly you see that myth as central to your work and also as central to our experience in America.

**MLS:** Well, it took a long time for me to realize that Antigone and

Creon need each other, that the balance point is between them. So neither one of them is right, and neither one is wrong. It's the tension between them that makes for a democratic system. If Creon wins, it's dictatorship; if Antigone wins, it's anarchy. It happens for me to be as essential a legend as there is about politics.

**BR:** Does that tension, that pull between Antigone and Creon, have to end in tragedy? Can it maintain a stasis, a balance?

**MLS:** Well, it hasn't ended in tragedy in this country; it only ended in tragedy in the myth, where she was immured. But I'm talking about the moment of the turning of the wrist. There's a line in the creed which says "eternally begotten of the Father." Eternally turning the wrist. The eternal No: just that point is where the tension lies. You know, in the eighteenth century there were two archetypal characters, Uncle Sam and Brother Jonathan. And Uncle Sam won. But, you see, he didn't win altogether, because in a way the Antigone-Creon myth is there as well. Are we a band of brothers, or do we have a paternal leader? We have daddy presidents all the time. Then we balance again and have a strong legislative band of brothers, and so it goes. American democracy is a fascinating revolutionary form of government. It always fails, and it always succeeds. It's crazy, isn't it?

**BR:** In this complex political and historical process you describe, how much control does any individual have? Johnny Church says a man can go with the tide, not rule it. Does this reflect the view in the quintet?

**MLS:** Yes, I think he has to be intelligent enough to know when the tide's coming in—the tide in the affairs of men that taken at the flood leads on to fortune. I think this is what Johnny meant. You go with the tide; you don't demand that the tide change.

**BR:** Do you believe one person can change history in important ways?

**MLS:** Yes, but the person who changes history sometimes in the most important ways of all is an unknown. Take Johnny and Thankful. They were the Agitators of a regiment that revolted against Cromwell. Their leader had been killed in a tavern. The Levellers were the left wing of the Parliamentary army and were so dangerous that they killed them off. Okay, what happened? Some of those men were sent to the colonies. The Commonwealth of Virginia is not called the commonwealth because of all this Cavalier nonsense they talk here. Virginia called itself a commonwealth. The language of those Levellers came over here, and there it was on Jefferson's ring. We may forget it, or try to forget it, but it's still there. It's still one of the impulses behind us.

**BR:** We keep coming back to *Prisons,* don't we?

**MLS:** Because essentially *Prisons* reverberates through the whole of the five volumes. There are different prisons of the South, prisons of the family, prisons of decision, and so on, that run all the way through. Johnny in the end of the book, Johnny who is killed in the drunk tank, is just as much a prisoner as the first Johnny.

**BR:** Is this why you've called *Prisons* your breakthrough novel?

**MLS:** I think that had to do not with any change in technique but with the depth, with what we were talking about earlier. You know, the ability to dive deeper, find out, face more.

**BR:** Clarity of vision.

**MLS:** That's exactly what we were talking about, about those moments or times in a novel or a poem when the fictional vision becomes a reality, when the language disappears and instead of standing back and intellectually judging it, you become, for a while, part of it. I think the whole of *Prisons* has it. Don't you?

# Selected Bibliography


## *Works by Mary Lee Settle*

*Blood Tie*. New York, 1978.
*Celebration*. New York, 1986.
*Charley Bland*. New York, 1989.
*The Clam Shell*. New York, 1971.
*Fight Night on a Sweet Saturday*. New York, 1964.
*The Killing Ground*. 1982; rpr. New York, 1988.
*The Kiss of Kin*. New York, 1955.
*Know Nothing*. 1960; rpr. New York, 1988.
*The Love Eaters*. New York, 1954.
*O Beulah Land*. 1956; rpr. New York, 1987.
*Prisons*. 1973; rpr. New York, 1987.
"Recapturing the Past in Fiction." *New York Times Book Review*, February 12, 1984, pp. 1, 36–37.
*The Scapegoat*. 1980; rpr. New York, 1988.
"The Search for Beulah Land." *Southern Review*, n.s., XXIV (1988), 13–26.

## *Works About Mary Lee Settle*

Allen, Bruce. Review of *The Killing Ground*. *Christian Science Monitor*, August 13, 1982, p. B-3.
Bach, Peggy. "The Searching Voice and Vision of Mary Lee Settle." *Southern Review*, n.s., XX (1984), 842–50.
Brown, Rosellen. Review of *The Scapegoat*. *New Republic*, December 27, 1980, p. 37.
Doctorow, E. L. Review of *The Scapegoat*. *New York Times Book Review*, October 26, 1980, pp. 1, 40–42.

Dyer, Joyce Coyne. "Mary Lee Settle's *Prisons:* Taproots History." *Southern Literary Journal,* XVII (1984), 26–39.

Garrett, George. "Mary Lee Settle." *Dictionary of Literary Biography,* 2nd ser. Detroit, 1980.

———. "Mary Lee Settle's Beulah Land Trilogy." In *Rediscoveries.* Edited by David Madden. New York, 1971.

———. *Understanding Mary Lee Settle.* Columbia, S.C., 1988.

Godwin, Gail. Review of *The Killing Ground. New Republic,* XVI (1982), 30–31.

Hart, Lyn. Review of *Know Nothing. Library Journal,* LXXXV (1960), 3105.

Hicks, Granville. Foreword to *O Beulah Land.* New York, 1965.

Houston, Robert. Review of *The Scapegoat. Nation,* November 8, 1980, pp. 469–71.

Joyner, Nancy Carol. "Mary Lee Settle's Connections: Class and Clothes in the Beulah Quintet." *Southern Quarterly,* XXII (1983), 33–45.

Peden, William. Review of *Know Nothing. Saturday Review,* November 5, 1960, p. 33.

Schafer, William J. "Mary Lee Settle's Beulah Quintet: History Darkly, Through a Single-Lens Reflex." *Appalachian Journal,* X (1982), 77–86.

Shattuck, Roger. Introduction to *The Beulah Quintet.* New York, 1981.

———. "A Talk with Mary Lee Settle." *New York Times Book Review,* October 26, 1980, pp. 43–46.

Swaim, Kathleen M. "A Fictional Gloss on the History of the 1640's." *Milton Quarterly,* XV (1981), 97–98.

Vance, Jane Gentry. "Historical Voices in Mary Lee Settle's *Prisons:* 'Too Far in Freedom.' " *Mississippi Quarterly,* XXXVIII (1985), 391–413.

———. "Mary Lee Settle's *The Beulah Quintet:* History Inherited, History Created." *Southern Literary Journal,* XVII (1984), 40–53.

## *Other Secondary Sources*

Armstrong, Nancy. *Desire and Domestic Fiction: A Political History of the Novel.* New York, 1987.

Barthes, Roland. *Image, Music, Text.* Translated by Stephen Heath. New York, 1977.

Baym, Nina. *Woman's Fiction: A Guide to Novels by and About Women in America, 1820–1870.* Ithaca, 1978.

Bennett, Arnold. *How to Become an Author.* London, 1903.

Carlyle, Thomas. *Selected Essays.* New York, 1972.

Clark, Robert. *History, Ideology, and Myth in American Fiction, 1823–52.* London, 1984.

Collingwood, R. G. *The Idea of History.* New York, 1946.

Dekker, George. *The American Historical Romance.* New York, 1987.

Douglas, Ann. *The Feminization of American Culture.* New York, 1977.

Eagleton, Terry. *Literary Theory: An Introduction.* Minneapolis, 1983.

Eco, Umberto. *A Theory of Semiotics.* Bloomington, 1976.

Eliot, George. *Essays.* Edited by Thomas Pinney. New York, 1963.

Fetherling, Dale. *Mother Jones: The Miners' Angel.* Carbondale, 1974.

Fisher, Philip. *Hard Facts: Setting and Form in the American Novel.* New York, 1985.

Fleishman, Avrom. *The English Historical Novel.* Baltimore, 1971.

Foley, Barbara. "From *U.S.A.* to *Ragtime:* Notes on the Forms of Historical Consciousness in Modern Fiction." *American Literature,* L (1978), 85–105.

———. *Telling the Truth: The Theory and Practice of Documentary Fiction*. Ithaca, 1986.

Foucault, Michel. *Discipline and Punish: The Birth of the Prison*. Translated by Alan Sheridan. New York, 1977.

———. *The Order of Things: An Archeology of the Human Sciences*. New York, 1970.

Fryer, Judith. *The Faces of Eve: Women in the Nineteenth-Century American Novel*. New York, 1976.

Gold, Michael. "Proletarian Realism." *New Masses,* VI (1930), 5.

Henderson, Harry B., III. *Versions of the Past: The Historical Imagination in American Fiction*. New York, 1974.

Hollowell, John. *Fact and Fiction: The New Journalism and the Nonfiction Novel*. Chapel Hill, 1977.

Iser, Wolfgang. *The Implied Reader: Patterns of Communication in Prose Fiction from Bunyan to Beckett*. Baltimore, 1974.

James, Henry. *Theory of Fiction*. Edited by James E. Miller, Jr. Lincoln, 1972.

LaCapra, Dominick. *History, Politics, and the Novel*. Ithaca, 1988.

Leisy, Ernest E. *The American Historical Novel*. Norman, 1950.

Lévi-Strauss, Claude. *Structural Anthropology*. Translated by Claire Jacobson and Brooke Grundfest Schoepf. New York, 1963.

Lukács, Georg. *The Historical Novel*. Translated by Hannah Mitchell and Stanley Mitchell. Boston, 1962.

Marcus, Steven. *Dickens: From Pickwick to Dombey*. New York, 1965.

McGann, Jerome J. *The Beauty of Inflections: Literary Investigations in Historical Method and Theory*. New York, 1988.

Overdyke, W. Darrell. *The Know-Nothing Party in the South*. Baton Rouge, 1950.

Rance, Nicholas. *The Historical Novel and Popular Politics in Nineteenth-Century England*. London, 1975.

Reynolds, David S. *Beneath the American Renaissance: The Subversive Imagination in the Age of Emerson and Melville*. New York, 1988.

Rideout, Walter. *The Radical Novel in the United States, 1900–1954*. Cambridge, Mass., 1956.

Schlesinger, Arthur, Jr. *The Cycles of American History*. Boston, 1986.

Shaw, Harry E. *The Forms of Historical Fiction: Sir Walter Scott and His Successors*. Ithaca, 1983.

Spears, Monroe K. *American Ambitions: Selected Essays on Literary and Cultural Themes*. Baltimore, 1987.

Uglow, Jennifer. *George Eliot*. New York, 1987.

White, Hayden. *The Content of the Form: Narrative Discourse and Historical Representation*. Baltimore, 1987.

Willey, Basil. *Nineteenth Century Studies: Coleridge to Matthew Arnold*. New York, 1949.

# Index